The Secret Thoughts of an Unlikely Convert

Praise for
The Secret Thoughts of an Unlikely Convert

As you read Champagne Butterfield's incredibly poignant and vulnerable account, you can't help but put yourself in Smith's place.... Would you have reached out to a woman who thought Christians and their God were "stupid, pointless and menacing"?

—Jim Daly, president, *Focus on the Family*,
www.crosswalk.com/blogs/jim-daly/the-power-of-our-words.html

There are some stories that just need to be told—some testimonies of the Lord's grace that are so unusual and so encouraging that they will bless everyone who hears them. This is exactly the case with Rosaria Butterfield, who recently authored *The Secret Thoughts of an Unlikely Convert*.

—Tim Challies, challies.com

The conversion that deconstructed her life and worldview taught her a thing or two about how Christians fail homosexuals and post-moderns. One such failure is an unbelief in Christ's power to transform people and the Bible's power to captivate people.

—Rev. Chuck Huckaby, worldviewchurch.org

Every now and then you read something that not only is a good book, but makes you want to have a meal with the author and get to know them better. This was one for me.

—Aimee Byrd, housewifetheologian.com

It's a fascinating, gritty glimpse into an intersection of unlikely worldviews.

—Mike Duran, mikeduran.com

The Secret Thoughts of an Unlikely Convert

an english professor's journey into christian faith

expanded edition

Rosaria Champagne Butterfield

Crown & Covenant
PUBLICATIONS

© 2014 by Rosaria Champagne Butterfield,
Crown & Covenant Publications
7408 Penn Avenue
Pittsburgh, PA 15208
www.crownandcovenant.com

Second Edition
Fifteenth Printing 2019

ISBN: 978-1-884527-80-7
ePub: 978-1-884527-81-4
Kindle: 978-1-884527-82-1

Library of Congress Control Number: 2013949580

Printed in the United States of America

The publisher has abbreviated or altered several names in this book to protect the privacy of certain individuals.

Cover and graphics by Ariana Davenport Stitzer. Text is set in Stemple Garamond and headers in Goodfish. Back cover photograph of Rosaria by Neil Boyd Photography, Raleigh, N.C. Photograph on page 151 by Isaac Pockras. Photograph on page 160 by Gary Fong, Genesis Photo Agency.

Unless otherwise indicated, all Scripture references taken from the New King James Version®. Copyright © 1982 by Thomas Nelson, Inc. Used by permission. All rights reserved.

Contents

Foreword

A re you an evangelical?" The voice on the phone pressed on. "What do you believe about the Bible?"

I had written her a letter inquiring about how such as I, a local pastor, could be sure that the university students in our city at least knew what the Bible says, regardless of whether or not they believed it. As a professor in the English department, she was responding. But I was surprised by her questions. She was—a fact I learned later—interviewing me!

The questions and dialogue on the phone continued for some time. It was friendly interchange, and with the next question I posed this response: "Dr. Champagne, I think that question should be considered in front of our fireplace following one of my wife's good dinners. How does that sound?"

She enthusiastically responded, "That sounds wonderful!" And so began a friendship which my wife and I have treasured and regarded as a gift from God.

It wasn't long before Rosaria was frequenting our table, always bringing something: cheese, freshly baked bread, and always an eager mind. What great conversations we had! As an English major in college, I relished these discussions with someone so cognizant of current authors. But much of our conversation related to the topics about which we had first spoken: the Bible, theology, and worldviews. She became very dear to us.

What follows is her story. From our early acquaintance, I recognized that our new friend feared no topic, spoke her mind in clear terms, and opened her heart as well as her thoughts. You will find that about her not only because that's the way she is, but also because that is who she is.

Our church in Syracuse had prayed for years for the university. Rosaria is one of God's gracious answers!

—*Kenneth G. Smith*

Acknowledgments
God, Why Pick Me?

When I was 28 years old, I boldly declared myself lesbian. I was at the finish of a PhD in English Literature and Cultural Studies. I was a teaching associate in one of the first and strongest women's studies departments in the nation. I was being recruited by universities to take on faculty and administrative roles in advancing radical leftist ideologies. I genuinely believed that I was helping to make the world a better place.

At the age of 36, I was one of the few tenured women at a large research university, a rising administrator, and a community activist. I had become one of the "tenured radicals." By all standards, I had made it. That same year, Christ claimed me for himself and the life that I had known and loved came to a humiliating end.

I am often asked to share my spiritual journey. People are interested to know what it is like to travel a long journey to Christ. I am not hesitant to oblige. How our lives bear the fruit of Christ's spilled blood is important. The stories of our lives can serve to encourage and warn others. But telling the stories of our lives is heady business. How and why are our stories shared? Are they shared to bring attention to ourselves? To shock people? To entertain?

Are our testimonies honoring to the whole landscape of the Christian journey? Not if they speak only of the "how-shocking-was-my-sin-before-I-met-the-Lord" story. (As though the sin I commit today is less shocking!) Not if they share only the safe feelings, rehearsed responses, and good "decisions" for which we give ourselves unearned credit.

My Christian memoir divulges the secret thoughts of an unlikely convert like me. This book seeks to uncover the hidden
landscape of the Christian life in its whole context, warts and
all. Perhaps some of my unrehearsed thoughts will resonate
with you. I often wonder: God, why pick me? I didn't ask to
be a Christian convert. I didn't "seek the Lord." Instead, I ran
like the wind when I suspected someone would start peddling
the gospel to me. I was intellectually—and only intellectually—
interested in matters of faith and I wanted to keep it that way.
How did a smart cookie like me end up in a place like this?

In the pages that follow, I share what happened in my private
world through what Christians politely call conversion. This
word—conversion—is simply too tame and too refined to cap-
ture the train wreck that I experienced in coming face-to-face
with the Living God. I know of only one word to describe this
time-released encounter: impact. Impact is, I believe, the space
between the multiple car crash and the body count. I try, in the
pages that follow, to relive the impact of God on my life.

I began this book in 2003. Although this book called me to
look back, each page is indelibly inscribed by the joyful demands of my day-to-day life. My husband, Kent, sacrificially
committed himself to helping me complete this project. Kent's
love, guidance, and support brought this book into light. Each
chapter collided with a child placed into our family through
adoption or foster care. And each chapter was punctuated by
the absence of other children, those whom I came to know
through desperate phone calls from the Department of Family Services; those whose needs or numbers exceeded our arms'
expanse. At each child's placement into our family, my mother
and stepfather, Dolores and Theo Otis, gave me all of the support and encouragement that I would need. I'm the only mother
that I know whose own mother single-handedly threw a progressive baby shower for each baby or child. With each gift for a
child, my mom always slipped in something wonderful for me.
("Rosaria, get your hair cut; get a pedicure; buy a new TV!")
The grafting of my children into my family with Kent, and the
grafting of my mother and stepfather into my present life, made
it safe for me to take the long look back that the writing of this
book required.

I wish to thank those who read and commented on many chapters: Kent Butterfield, Pastor Bruce and Kim Backensto, Pastor Doug and Amy Comin, Natalie Gazo, and Pastor Ken and Floy Smith. All of the errors in judgment and offenses that you find on these pages, however, are solely mine.

I also wish to thank those people who supported and encouraged me during the writing of this book by their words, examples, and teaching: Pastor Charles and Margaret Biggs, Pastor Steve and Julie Bradley, Matthew Filbert, Pastor Jerry and Ann O'Neill, Dolores and Theo Otis.

God used the unsuspecting members of the Syracuse Reformed Presbyterian Church in countless ways. I am indebted to: Pastor Brian and Dorian Coombs, Phyllis Coombs, Kurt and Kathy Donath, George and Maggie Hueber, Chris and Shari Huggins, Gene and Gail Huggins, M and NM, Bob and Vivian Rice, Ben and Diana Rice, Dr. Ken and Becky Smith, Dr. Jonathan and Marty Wright, and Ron and Robyn Zorn.

I also thank my colleagues and friends from Geneva College, especially Dr. Byron Curtis, Dr. Dean Smith, Dr. Bob Frazier, Dr. Maureen Vanterpool, Dr. Jonathan Watt, and President Emeritus Jack White; I thank my mentor and boss from the Center for Urban Biblical Ministry, Mrs. Karla Threadgill Byrd.

Finally, memoirs collide past and present in messy and bizarre ways. My colleagues and friends from my Classical Conversations Homeschool Community in Purcellville, Virginia, keep a smile on my face, a spring in my step, and a Latin verb to conjugate on the tip of my tongue. I am honored to share the daily trench of homeschooling with Regina Gossage, Alissa Hall, Martha Mason, Julia Shaw-Fuller, and Jennifer Truesdale. My editor at Crown & Covenant Publications, Lynne Gordon, is the most compassionate reader in my world, and I thank her for her interest in this book and for the myriad of ways that she improved it.

I am grateful to the Reformed Presbyterian Church of North America, and to the pastors, sessions, and members who have sacrificed their time, money, and personal liberty for Christ's covenant. I am grateful for the denomination's historical and bold stand for abolition and for the example of Christ-commanded racial advocacy that this sets for us today.

I dedicate this book to my children, in the hopes that they each will write their own worldview testimony for God's saving grace through Christ Jesus, our Lord.

1

Conversion and the Gospel of Peace

Syracuse, N.Y., 1997–2000

How do I tell you about my conversion to Christianity without making it sound like an alien abduction or a train wreck? Truth be told, it felt like a little of both. The language normally used to describe this odd miracle does not work for me. I didn't read one of those tacky self-help books with a thin coating of Christian themes, examine my life against the tenets of the Bible the way one might hold up one car insurance policy against all others and cleanly and logically "make a decision for Christ." While I did make choices along the path of this journey, they never felt logical, risk-free, or sane. Neither did I feel like the victim of an emotional/spiritual earthquake and collapse gracefully into the arms of my Savior, like a holy and sanctified Scarlett O'Hara having been "claimed by Christ's irresistible grace." Heretical as it might seem, Christ and Christianity seemed eminently resistible.

My Christian life unfolded as I was just living my life, my normal life. In the normal course of life questions emerged that exceeded my secular feminist worldview. Those questions sat quietly in the crevices of my mind until I met a most unlikely friend: a Christian pastor. Had a pastor named Ken Smith not shared the gospel with me for years and years, over and over again, not in some used-car-salesman way, but in an organic, spontaneous and compassionate way, those questions might still be lodged in the crevices of my mind and I might never have met the most unlikely of friends, Jesus Christ himself.

It is dangerous to look back on my life, from the perspective of a lover and follower of Christ, now also a wife and a mother. It is painful to lay my hand on the absence of my former life, and breathe. My former life still lurks in the edges of my heart, shiny and still like a knife.

I come to the limits of language when I try to describe my life in Jesus Christ.

My life as I knew it became train wrecked in April 1999, at the age of 36—just a few weeks shy of 37. At that time, I was an associate professor at Syracuse University, recently tenured in the English Department, also holding a joint teaching appointment in the Center for Women's Studies. I was in a lesbian relationship with a woman who was primarily an animal activist and a nature lover and also an adjunct professor at a neighboring university. Together we owned homes, cohabitating both in life and in the university's domestic partnership policy. My partner T ran a business: she rehabilitated abused and abandoned Golden Retrievers for placement as helper dogs for the disabled or family dogs for those animals not strong enough to work. Our houses (we owned and lived in two—one in the country and one in the university district) were hubs of intellectual and activist work. Aside from the kennel, we supported a lot of causes: AIDS health care, children's literacy, sexual abuse healing, and disability activism. We were members of a Unitarian Universalist Church, where I was the coordinator of what is called the Welcoming Committee, the gay and lesbian advocacy group.

My historical field in English studies was 19th century literature and culture. My historical interests in 19th century literature were grounded in the philosophical and political worldviews of Freud, Marx, and Darwin. My primary field was Critical Theory—also known as postmodernism. My specialty was Queer Theory (a postmodern form of gay and lesbian studies). In my department, tenure requirements were rigorous, expecting a published and reviewed book, six scholarly articles, and significant exposure at conferences, delivering lectures on the topic of your research. I remember thinking that this intensity of intellectual work was normal until I explained our department's tenure requirements to a doctor friend. He said, "Wow! That's like having to cut out your own spleen and eat it!" Albeit apparently toxic, my work, nonetheless, felt vital and enriching.

Looking back now, I don't know how to think about myself as a professor. Most often, I felt like an impostor—I felt like I wasn't really smart enough to be there. I always felt lucky to get a job at Syracuse University. I didn't assume I would get tenure there and was a little surprised that I did.

Within three years I became the Director of Undergraduate Studies and I enjoyed advising and organizing our curriculum and encouraging our students. Some of my senior colleagues advised me against becoming a department administrator before I received tenure, not only because administrative work would take time away from my research and writing, but also because administrators get embroiled in department politics where it is easy to make gratuitous enemies and hard to recover lost ground. I rejected this traditional counsel and took the job anyway. In bucking the traditional advice, I learned a good lesson: Success comes when we build on our strengths. Doing something I loved and I was good at helped me to get my writing and research done in an efficient and focused way. Although risky, working from my strengths turned out to be a good risk and I'm glad that I took it. I felt vindicated in the principle that risks are worth taking and that gain is only sweet when you actually have something to lose.

In spite of feeling like an impostor, I apparently didn't look like one. I did a lot of high-profile things as a professor. I gave a keynote address at a gay pride march and was invited by major universities, including Harvard University, to lecture on gay and lesbian studies. I tried to do my work with integrity and enthusiasm, but certain aspects of my job were hard for me, like working with graduate students on their dissertations and comprehensive exams. The job market was always bad and I never really felt equipped to mentor their research.

The part of my job that I loved the best was undergraduate teaching. I still shiver at the dynamism and the epiphanies of the classroom. I miss this. I also miss my colleagues. I miss being in the company of risky and complex thinkers, people who are invested in our culture and who challenge me to think to the edges of my comfort zones. I believed then and I believe now that where everybody thinks the same nobody thinks very much. I miss being around people who find their equilibrium in contradiction and diversity. Of course, there were other perks—a dependable salary, the best job security in the world, tuition remission for my family members at Syracuse University and research universities of equivalent status, a great research budget, a book budget, opportunity to travel. But even now, homeschooling two of our four children and living on one salary, I don't miss the material benefits. I miss the people.

As a lesbian activist, I was *involved* in my gay community. I had drafted and lobbied for the university's first successful domestic partnership policy, which gives spousal benefits to gay couples. I had to put up with a lot of flak from the conservative Christian community for this. My life was busy and full, and, I thought, moral. I was concerned with issues of morality, and even authored an article on the subject of the morality of gay and lesbian lives. I was an "out" lesbian in the same way that I am now an "out" Christian. It would never occur to me to live my life in falsehood, and I had and have the kind of privileged jobs (then as a professor and now as a Christian wife) where I do not have to be "careful" or closeted. The closest I ever got to Christians during these times were students who refused to read material in university classrooms on the grounds that "knowing Jesus" meant never needing to know anything else; people who sent me hate mail; or people who carried signs at gay pride marches that read "God Hates Fags." (By the way, "God Hates Fags" is also a website where young nominally Christian homophobes can log on to acquire hate tactics.)

Christians always seemed like bad thinkers to me. It seemed that they could maintain their worldview only because they were sheltered from the world's real problems, like the material structures of poverty and violence and racism. Christians always seemed like bad readers to me, too. They appeared to use the Bible in a way that Marxists would call "vulgar"—that is, common, or in order to bring the Bible into a conversation to stop the conversation, not deepen it. "The Bible says" always seemed to me like a mantra that invited everyone to put his or her brain on hold. "The Bible says" was the Big Pause before the conversation stopped. Their catch phrases and clichés were (and are) equally off-putting. "Jesus is the answer" seemed to me then and now like a tree without a root. Answers come after questions, not before. Answers answer questions in specific and pointed ways, not in sweeping generalizations. "It's such a blessing" always sounds like a violation of the Third Commandment ("Do not take the Lord's name in vain") or a Hallmark card drunk with schmaltz. It seemed to me that the only people who could genuinely be satisfied with this level of reading and thinking were people who didn't really read or think very much—about life or culture or anything.

In addition to appearing to be anti-intellectual, Christians also scared me. Outside of the Lord, life is a very treacherous ordeal. Proverbs teaches this when its author Solomon writes: "The way of the unfaithful is hard" (Prov. 13:15). Of course, Christian life is hard too, but it is hard in another way, in a way that is at least bearable and purposeful. Christians can lay hold of the meaning and purpose and grace of suffering and truly believe that all things, even the evil ones, "work together for good for those who love God, to those who are called according to his purpose" (Rom. 8:28). A life outside of Christ is both hard and frightening; a life in Christ has hard edges and dark valleys, but it is purposeful even when painful.

I get ahead of myself. Here is one of the deepest ways Christians scared me: The lesbian community was home and home felt safe and secure; the people that I knew the best and cared about were in that community; and finally, the lesbian community was accepting and welcoming while the Christian community appeared (and too often is) exclusive, judgmental, scornful, and afraid of diversity. What also scared me is that, while Christianity seemed like just another worldview, this one for people who enjoyed living narrowly circumscribed lives, Christians claimed that their worldview and all of the attending features that I saw— Republican politics, homeschooling biases, refusal to inoculate children against childhood illnesses, etc.—had God on its side.

Christians still scare me when they reduce Christianity to a lifestyle and claim that God is on the side of those who attend to the rules of the lifestyle they have invented or claim to find in the Bible.

Although I knew that I wasn't the smartest scholar in my department, I enjoyed doing research and writing. I enjoyed (and still do) the risk of examining new ideas. I had a sticky note on my computer with a quotation whose author I never knew. It read: "I would rather be wrong on an important point than right on a trivial one." This quotation reminded me that when you make your mistakes in public you will learn that they are mistakes and in being corrected you will grow. It also reminded me that being wrong and responding to correction with resilience was a higher virtue than covering up your mistakes so your students and the watching world assumed that success meant never being wrong. Working from your strengths and cultivating resilience in all matters of life have always been guiding principles for me.

I'm a former gymnast and marathon runner, and I have always found flexibility and a steady pace to be more useful than perfection or bursts of speed. Winners have always seemed to me people who know how to fall on their face, pick themselves up, and recover well. It has always seemed to me that without the proper response to failure, we don't grow, we only age. So I was and am willing to take the risk of being wrong for the hope of growing in truth. It seemed to me that if we fall, we need to fall forward and not backward, because at least then we are moving in the right direction. Resilience, recovery, and recognition of my strengths and failures galvanized my research and my life.

In spite of having a worldview that valued flexibility, unanswerable Big Life Questions started to nag at me while I was doing initial research and writing for my second book, a study of the rise of the Religious Right in America, and the hermeneutic of hatred that the Religious Right uses against their favorite target: queers, or at that time, people like me. I had been studying the Christian Right since 1992, since Pat Robertson at the 1992 Republican National Convention declared: "Feminism encourages women to leave their husbands, kill their children, practice witchcraft, destroy capitalism, and become lesbians." I thought then, and I think now, that this is a foolish and a dangerous statement. After all, it was the first wave of feminism in this country that secured for women the right to vote and access to public education. It seemed to me then and it seems to me now that Christians truly become ugly when we become jealous of the successful persuasive rhetoric of others. The truth is, feminists have been more successful rhetoricians at the core of major U.S. universities than have Christians, even though most of these universities have Christian origins.

Although I live my life now for Christ and Christ alone, I do not find myself in like-minded company when my fellow Christians bemoan the state of the university today. Feminism has a better reputation than Christianity at all major U.S. universities and this fact really bothers (and confuses) many Christians. Feminism has truly captured the soul of secular U.S. universities and the church has either been too weak or too ignorant to know and to know better. But how has the church responded to this truth? Too often the church sets itself up as a victim of this paradigm shift in America, but I think this is dishonest. Here's what I think happened: Since all major U.S. universities had Christian roots, too many Christians thought that they could rest in Christian tradition, not Christian relevance. Too often the church does not know how to interface with university culture because it comes to the table only ready to moralize and not dialogue. There is a core difference between sharing the gospel with the lost and imposing a specific moral standard on the unconverted. Like it or not, in the court of public opinion, feminists and not Bible-believing Christians have won the war of intellectual integrity. And Christians are in part to blame for this.

The Pat Robertson quotation is a good example of what I saw in my study of the Religious Right (and what I still see): spiritual pride and club Christianity. But I also knew that there was more to it than that. I wondered about this. What is the core of Christianity? Why do true believers believe? What do they believe? Why is their faith person-centered and not idea-centered? Because I'm an English professor, I had to read the Bible to make sense of the hermeneutic used by the Christian Right. Because I was a scholar, I knew that, without having studied Hebrew or Greek, or knowing the relationship between the different fields of theology and different applications of doctrine, canon, and textual study, I was not able to study the Bible on my own. I started a self-study of Greek and searched for someone to help me understand the Bible. "Help" came in a most unusual way.

After I published in the local newspaper a critique of the Promise Keepers for their gender politics, I received a batch of mail: hate mail and fan mail. I received so many letters for this little editorial that I kept empty Xerox paper boxes on both sides of my desk, one for hate mail and one for fan mail. (Oh, how I wished people would have read my recently-gone-into-paperback-tenure-book with the same gusto!) In this batch of mail, I also received a letter from Pastor Ken Smith, then-pastor of the Syracuse Reformed Presbyterian Church. It was a kind and inquiring letter. It encouraged me to explore the kind of questions I admire: How did you arrive at your interpretations? How do you know you are right? Do you believe in God? He didn't argue with my article; he asked me to explore and defend the presuppositions that undergirded it. I didn't really know how to respond to Ken's letter, but I found myself reading and re-reading it. I didn't know which box to file this letter in, and so it sat on my desk and haunted me.

After many days of thinking about this, Ken's letter made me confront the presuppositional problem of my research: As an intellectual, I was working from a historical materialist worldview, but Christianity was essentially a supernatural worldview. Christians maintained that Jesus Christ was historically and globally true, but his entrance into history violated a core value of my research: No one, according to the tenets of historical materialism, enters history; rather, we all emerge from it. The "who, what, why, and how" of Jesus Christ is a great mystery. I had never thought about presuppositional questions that were supernatural or spiritual in nature, and yet here I was embarking on a writing project that made me confront this worldview-divide. Pastor Ken's letter punctured the integrity of my research project without him even knowing it!

It may seem strange to you, but no one had asked me those questions before or led me to ask them of myself. These were reasonable questions, but not the sort of questions that postmodern professors toss around at faculty meetings or the local bar. The Bible makes it clear that reason is not the front door of faith. It takes spiritual eyes to discern spiritual matters. But how do we develop spiritual eyes unless Christians engage the culture with those questions and paradigms of mindfulness out of which spiritual logic flows? That's exactly what Ken's letter did for me—invited me to think in ways I hadn't before.

By the way, I hate a messy desk, one where papers litter the surface. Pastor Ken's letter sat on my desk for a whole week— this is six days longer than I can normally stand. It really bothered me that I didn't know where to file it. I threw it away a few times but always found myself digging through the department's recycling bin to reclaim it at the day's end. It was a careful letter, two pages in length, written on church stationery. It was neatly typed and Pastor Ken's signature was bold and clear. The name of the church was Syracuse Reformed Presbyterian Church and I assumed that "reformed" implied a critique of tradition-for-tradition's sake. From his signature and some of the language he used I assumed that Pastor Ken was old but not priggish. The letter invited me to call its author to discuss these ideas more fully. It was the kindest letter of opposition that I had ever received. After a week, I called.

We had a nice chat on the phone, and Pastor Ken invited me to dinner at his house to explore some of these questions. Before we ended our phone call, almost as an afterthought, Pastor Ken also said that if I was afraid to come to some stranger's home that he and his wife would meet me at a restaurant. I thought that that was very considerate of him—almost chivalrous! I was comfortable with the idea of going to his house. The gay and lesbian community is also a community "given to hospitality." I honed my hospitality gifts serving pasta to drag queens and queers—people like me. I prefer discussing matters of disagreement around a private table. Plus I really wanted to see how Christians lived! I had never seen such a thing! So I took him up on it. I was excited to meet a real born-again Christian and find out why he believed such silly ideas. I assumed that this dinner was another aspect of my research. Pastor Ken lived about two miles from my house, his house also in the university district. I knew exactly where he lived—in fact, his house was on my running route—so I wasn't too nervous about this first meeting. I went alone.

I remember in great detail that first meeting with Ken and his wife, Floy. I remember being conscious of my butch haircut and the gay and pro-choice bumper stickers on my car. I remember how relieved I was when I learned that Floy made a vegetarian stir fry for supper. (I tried to maintain a vegetarian diet for health as well as for moral reasons.) I remember awkwardly greeting my hosts at the door and pulling out of my bag two gifts—a bottle of good red wine and a box of strong tea. It was a hot July day and I was glad that they didn't use air conditioning (I was concerned about the environment in general and the ozone layer in particular and assumed that they were, too). I share with you these details because they reflect my thinking at the time. I wanted to get to know these people but not at the expense of compromising my moral standards. My lesbian identity and culture and its values mattered a lot to me. I came to my culture and its values through life experience but also through much research and deep thinking. I liked Ken and Floy immediately because they seemed sensitive to that. Even though obviously these Christians and I were very different, they seemed to know that I wasn't just a blank slate, that I had values and opinions too, and they talked with me in a way that didn't make me feel erased.

The most memorable part of this meal was Ken's prayer before the meal. I had never heard anyone pray to God as if God cared, as if God listened, and as if God answered. It was not a pretentious prayer uttered for the heathen at the table to overhear. (I have heard a few of those at gay pride marches or in front of Planned Parenthood clinics.) It was a private and honest utterance, and I felt as though I was treading on something real, something sincere, something important, and something transparent but illegible to me. Ken made himself vulnerable to me in his prayer by humbling himself before this "God" of his, and I took note of that. During our meal I remember holding my breath and waiting to be punched in the stomach with something grossly offensive. I believed at this time that God was dead and that if he ever was alive, the fact of poverty, violence, racism, sexism, homophobia, and war was proof that he didn't care about his creation. I believed that religion was, as Marx wrote, the opiate of the masses, an imperialist social construction made to soothe the existential angst of the intellectually impaired. But Ken's God seemed alive, three-dimensional and wise, if firm. And Ken and Floy were anything but intellectually impaired.

Our conversation was lively and fun. If Floy was a "submissive wife" she was also gifted, smart, perceptive, well-read, and a great cook! If Ken was the "Bible-thumping" pastor, he was also a good listener, a balanced interpreter, a lover of good poetry, a reader of culture and politics, and a husband who clearly adored, relied upon, and valued highly his wife's counsel. These people simply didn't fit the stereotype and I simply didn't know what to do with this. Like his letter, Ken wouldn't be filed away easily so that I could just go on with my life.

Ken and Floy did something at the meal that has a long Christian history but has been functionally lost in too many Christian homes. Ken and Floy invited the stranger in—not to scapegoat me, but to listen and to learn and to dialogue. Ken and Floy have a vulnerable and transparent faith. We didn't debate worldview; we talked about our personal truth and about what "made us tick." Ken and Floy didn't identify with me. They listened to me and identified with Christ. They were willing to walk the long journey to me in Christian compassion. During our meal, they did not share the gospel with me. After our meal, they did not invite me to church. Because of these glaring omissions to the Christian script as I had come to know it, when the evening ended and Pastor Ken said he wanted to stay in touch, I knew that it was truly safe to accept his open hand.

Since this beginning, the journey on which the Lord has taken me has been a great adventure, and this simple meal in a pastor's home, the unlikely circle made by a radical lesbian feminist professor and two strong Christians in their 70s, a heavy Syracuse sun setting as we talked behind a large wall of windows in their home, was the first leg of this journey. I left their table needing to know a number of things: Does God exist? If God does exist, what does he expect from me? How do I communicate with him? How do I know who he is and what he wants? What if God is dead? Do I have the courage to face the truth, either way?

Before I ever set foot in a church, I spent two years meeting with Ken and Floy and on and off "studying" Scripture and my heart. If Ken and Floy had invited me to church at that first meal I would have careened like a skateboard off a cliff, and would have never come back. Ken, of course, knows the power of the word preached but it seemed to me he also knew at that time that I couldn't come to church—it would have been too threatening, too weird, too much. So, Ken was willing to bring the church to me. This gave me the room and the safety that I needed to match Ken and Floy's vulnerability and transparency. And so I opened up to them. I let them know who I was and what I valued. I invited them into my home and into my world. They met my friends, came to my dinner parties, saw me function in my real life. They made themselves safe enough for me to do this.

At the beginning of any project, I read and reread the book that I am trying to understand. At this point, I read and re-read the Bible. I read it voraciously and compulsively—as I do all books. I spent about five hours each day reading the Bible. I read every translation I could acquire—including the Catholic Bible. I still thought I was doing research for a book on the Religious Right. Ken and Floy, during those two years, asked me questions about my reading and my observations, but didn't pressure me or push me or interfere in my life. They were just there. If a month or two went by and I hadn't responded to Ken's e-mail inquiry or phone call, he would pop over to my house, like any neighbor might do, bringing greetings or a book or a loaf of homemade bread. Ken and Floy and I became friends. My father died when I was 22. I found myself trusting Ken the way that I had imagined myself as a grown woman trusting my own deceased dad.

After we had been meeting for a while, Ken approached me with a proposition: How about if he, Pastor Ken Smith, had a chance to speak to my English majors about why the Bible is a foundational book for English majors to read? He explained that he had a lecture already written and that he had delivered it successfully before. Clearly, he reasoned, as I was now reading the Bible, I could tell that it was filled with every literary genre and much literary merit. I remember being intrigued at what his lecture might contain but also remember feeling like a full-on threatened Mama Bear at even the hint that I would let this evangelical Christian have at my English majors! I was the gatekeeper and I didn't want my students hearing something that would undermine what we all had been teaching them. So I told Ken no, firmly and definitively. And then I asked Ken how he would feel about having an audience of one for this lecture—me. Much to my surprise, he took me up on it.

Ken and Floy came over for dinner to give me this lecture on the Bible. I invited them on a night when I was sure to be alone in the house. I think I served tofu and brown rice and broccoli and peach tea. I still have the scribbles on the legal pad that Ken used as he lectured. He gave an impressive overview of all the 66 texts that make up the Bible. His focus was on redemption—on how the Old Testament concealed the cross and the New Testament revealed it. His point of contact was Calvary and it made me think for the first time about what Jesus had endured at Calvary. Ken did a lot of talking at this lecture—he had a lot of material to cover. I was both intrigued and infuriated. The more he talked, the more infuriated I became. If what this guy said was true, then everything that I believed—every jot and tittle—was false!

At the end—which, by the way, I thought would never come— he said, "What do you think?" I said something like, "You have one book that claims itself to be true, which is in philosophy called an ontological fallacy, and I have about fifty on my shelf that say you're wrong. So it all comes down to how and why you claim that the Bible is true." I hoped this would burst his bubble and send him packing and out the door. But it didn't. Ken clapped his hands with a big toothy smile that seemed to imply that we were on the same page. (We were not.) He said with great joy and delight, "Exactly!" Ken's enthusiasm for opposition annoyed me to no end.

We agreed that next time he would tell me how and why the Bible is true.

This seemed so naive and so preposterous. I was a product of a postmodern education. There are no truths, only truth claims. After Ken and Floy left, I took a long walk with my dog Murphy. Walking in the cold dark, I thought about how peaceful life would be if I really believed that there was a knowable, dependable, sturdy, and comprehensive idea of truth and a man-God who so loved his people that he endured the wrath of God the Father for the sins that I had committed and those I would go on to commit. But even this train of thought was not comforting to me. After all, what would I do with my past? I surely couldn't throw it all away. My past was my shrine and any person or worldview that entered into my little world had to genuflect to this. I wondered about these Christians. Surely some of them had pasts. What did they do? How did they let go of their past without losing their identity? Who would I be without my lesbian identity? Of course, I had not always been a lesbian. But once I had my first girlfriend, I was hooked and I was sure I found my "real" self. Still, I wondered about this God who died for the sins of his people. It sounded too good to be true. I allowed myself to wonder if it could possibly be true. This self-question gave me a frightening pause.

Was I losing myself? Was I losing my mind?

A few weeks later Ken came over to my house with a book on Christian education and I was out running. I felt kind of embarrassed that he met my lesbian partner. Even though we had been meeting for over a year, I had kept T hidden. It was the first time that I ever felt anything but pride in "who I was."

From April of 1997 to February of 1999 I read the Bible, (mostly) enjoyed talking with Ken and Floy, and (mostly) enjoyed turning over these new ideas. If I started to struggle with something, or started to face a word like "sin" or "repentance," I quickly pushed it aside and read on.

I felt like a bonafide liberal, having friends who were so different from me! I felt like, on the liberal front, I had finally arrived! Ken would come to campus a lot and he and I continued to debate one another on panels discussing things like patriarchy or Promise Keepers. Some of my graduate students thought he was dangerous but I thought he was safe in a dangerous way. They said I was splitting hairs and losing my objectivity. I reminded them that I was a postmodernist who didn't believe in objectivity.

One thing that made Ken safe as well as dangerous was a point of commonality between us. We both are good teachers. Good teachers make it possible for people to change their positions without shame. Even as Ken prayed for my soul, he did it in a way that welcomed me into the church rather than made me a scapegoat of Christian fear or an example of what not to become.

One thing that really struck me about Ken and Floy's character during these years was how unselfish they were. I observed that they fed and housed and counseled countless people from all walks of life. I saw how wide the door to their home and the door to their heart opened. I remember feeling like I could talk to them about anything. Ken stressed that he accepted me as a lesbian but that he didn't approve of me as a lesbian. He held that line firmly and I appreciated that. I had a whole university of approving people so I didn't feel that I needed his, too. I learned that their eldest son, Dr. Ken Smith, was a colleague of mine at Syracuse. Oddly, we were on an important all-university committee together, the Budget Committee. I had thought that Dr. Ken was the only one on the committee who had a clue about what was going on. (I surely knew that I didn't.) The Budget Committee was an important committee because it gave the current administration a time to check out those professors who had been selected to become future deans and presidents. They could watch and groom and invent us. Of course this is one of the many little open secrets of the life of a professor, but secret or not, it was gospel and we all knew it. We were being watched, we were being groomed, and some of us would go places. Dr. Ken and I had also experienced "professor camp" together—a weeklong seminar in the Adirondacks—during black fly season!—where we were indoctrinated by the administration into the latest teaching fad.

Dr. Ken, seeing me struggle with the Budget Committee work, became an accounting tutor and big brother of sorts. I thought that odd but helpful. With these Christians in my life, certain aspects of my life had started to lose the sharp edges that it had before. With these Christians in my life, my life became a little kinder and a little safer.

One night Ken and Floy introduced me to a man named R. He was a former sex addict and heavy drug user. He also was Italian and had an English degree from Berkeley. We had much in common. I was drawn to him immediately. He worked at the university also and had come to a number of my lectures, unbeknownst to me. We became fast friends. R shared the gospel with great spontaneity and relevance. He would soon become my link to the church.

During this time, I thought about going to Ken's church—I thought that it would be good for my research and I also thought that it would be interesting. What did they do there at this Reformed Presbyterian Church? I wondered. Did they speak in tongues? Did they wail and weep and dance in the aisles? Sometimes I would get in my truck Sunday morning and try to drive to church. I would make it to the Cole Muffler parking lot next to church. I imagined how absurd my red truck with the gay rights bumper stickers and NARAL (National Abortion Rights Action League) support sticker would look in the church's parking lot, with all the minivans with stickers that read "Abortion stops a beating heart" and "Warning: un-socialized homeschoolers on board!" I figured that people probably didn't wear jeans, as I always did, and the women probably didn't wear a crew cut. Sometimes I would just sit there and read the *New York Times* and drink my Starbucks coffee and watch. I laughed out loud once realizing that I had become a church stalker! I did wonder about those large families pouring out of their minivans. I wondered who they were, what they struggled with, what substantive issues comprised their lives. I wondered how they could afford all those children.

During this time of struggle, others tried to help. A Methodist pastor and the Dean of the Chapel at Syracuse University believed that I did not have to give up everything to honor God. Indeed, he told me, since God made me a lesbian, I gave God honor by living an honorable lesbian life. He told me that I could have Jesus and my lesbian lover. This was a very appealing prospect. But I had been reading and rereading Scripture, and there are no such marks of postmodern "both/and" in the Bible. Plus, truth be told, I was getting tired of my relationship with T. Something in my value system was changing. While I continued to find T attractive, I no longer found her compelling. The things she cared about seemed shallow. I thought that maybe I was just bored.

My friends from the gay community were on the alert. On Thursday nights, I had a regular tradition: I made a big dinner and opened my home for anyone in the gay and lesbian community to come and eat and talk about issues and needs. This is important for professors and pastors alike to do, since both jobs put you out of reach from the very people you think that you know. A regular at these events was a transgendered woman, J, a dear friend of mine who lives full-time in drag—she is biologically male but lives full-time as a woman and has taken female hormones for long enough that she is now chemically castrated. I was in the kitchen and J came in to help. She told me point-blank that all this Bible reading was changing me, and she wanted to know, before any more pasta could be served or wine glasses filled, what was going on in my life.

At first I denied it, but she pressed. Finally, I said, "What would you say if I told you that I'm beginning to believe that Jesus is real, is a real and risen and loving and judging Lord, and that I am in big trouble?" She sat down at the kitchen stool, exhaled deeply, took my small hands in her large ones, and said, "Rosaria, I know that Jesus is a risen and living Lord. I was a Presbyterian minister for 15 years, and during that time, I prayed that the Lord would heal me. He didn't, but maybe he'll heal you. I'll pray for you."

The next day, when I came home from work, I found two milk crates over-filled with books: J gave me her library of theology. Just a few summers ago, when I read through John Calvin's *Institutes*, in pen, in my friend's handwriting, are cautions, notes to self: "Be careful here; don't forget Romans 1." Romans 1, especially verses 24-28, contains the most frightening lines in Scripture to anyone struggling in sexual sin:

> Therefore, God gave them over in the lusts of their hearts to impurity, so that their bodies would be dishonored among them.

> For they exchanged the truth of God for a lie, and worshipped and served the creature rather than the Creator, who is blessed forever, Amen.

> For this reason God gave them over to degrading passions; for their women exchanged the natural function for that which is unnatural.

> And in the same way also the men abandoned the natural function of the woman and burned in their desire toward one another, men with men committing indecent acts and receiving in their own persons the due penalty of their error.

> And just as they did not see fit to acknowledge God any longer, God gave them over to a depraved mind, to do those things which are not proper. (NASB)

Finally, my dear lesbian neighbor, a woman old enough to be my mother, as she was fond of reminding me, turned to me one morning as we were having coffee at my kitchen table before our weekly farmer's market journey, and said: "Why Jesus? Why not Buddha? Or Yoga? Why did you surrender your life to the God in whose name so much harm has been done to gay people?" Indeed. *Why Jesus?*

I was so tossed about by what I was hearing that I learned, in spite of my pride, to pray. I had stopped writing my book on the Religious Right because I couldn't talk myself into believing the things that I used to believe. I had been raised in the Catholic Church, and in spite of myself, I started to recall teachings and sensibilities that had once organized my childhood faith. I even started to bring to mind the Lord's Prayer and the Apostles' Creed, prayers and creeds that Catholics learn by heart and recite each Sunday.

I decided to put all of this before Ken Smith and see what he thought of my confused state. It was risky to do, but Ken was by now my friend. He was the only person in my life that could help me make sense of a spiritual crisis. Without an appointment, I showed up at the Syracuse Reformed Presbyterian Church and found Ken in his office. I sat down in his chair and said, "Ken, my whole world is turning upside down. What should I do?"

Ken listened. He didn't tell me what to do. Instead, he asked me a question. "Did you ever repudiate your Catholic background?"

His question intrigued me. (They always did.) I told him that I had never thought about it, that being Catholic was like being Italian for me. I told him that I didn't ever remember a time when I chose to be Catholic, but I clearly remember the time when I chose to walk away from the church—after my best friend confessed to having sex with our parish priest. Years later, I learned through a newspaper article that my mom found that Father P had had sex with a lot of children. The clincher was that Father P was the best priest I ever had and he taught me the most about God's commandments, law, and love. I felt the furious betrayal of a jilted believer. My feminist vocabulary gave me the words to articulate this fury: When God, Father, and Culture become bedfellows, patriarchy's danger is unleashed. That's how I called the game.

Ken listened deeply and was silent for a while. When he spoke he refocused me. He said, "No, I don't mean the church, I mean

God the Father, God the Son and God the Holy Spirit. Did you ever really repudiate the God outlined in the Apostles' Creed?"

I was stunned that he had mentioned the Apostles' Creed.

I told him that I had been reciting in my head that week the Lord's Prayer and the Apostles' Creed. I wasn't calling them to mind in an intentional way. They were just stuck in my head the same way that the theme song to the old 1970s TV show *Petticoat Junction* was stuck in my head for the first ten miles of my last marathon.

For someone raised Catholic, though, the church was God himself, so I never thought about separating the two. I never thought you could believe that the Apostles' Creed might be true and not be a member of the Catholic Church (the "one true Church" as the Catholic Church teaches). I also thought that the use of the word "catholic" in the Apostles' Creed meant the Catholic Church. Here is the Apostles' Creed as I had memorized it and as Catholics teach it:

> I believe in God, the Father Almighty, Creator of heaven and earth; and in Jesus Christ, his only Son, our Lord; who was conceived by the Holy Ghost, born of the Virgin Mary, suffered under Pontius Pilate, was crucified, died, and was buried. He descended into Hell; the third day he rose again from the dead; he ascended into heaven, sitteth at the right hand of God, the Father Almighty; from thence he shall come to judge the living and the dead. I believe in the Holy Ghost, the Holy Catholic Church, the communion of the saints, the forgiveness of sins, the resurrection of the body, and life everlasting. Amen. (*The Catholic Encyclopedia*, p. 14)

I never thought about "Holy Catholic Church" meaning the church universal, that is, all who call upon Christ for forgiveness of sins. I thought it meant the Catholic denomination.

Ken asked me another question.

"Have you ever repudiated your baptism?"

I said that I had never thought about my baptism, not once. My mom keeps in a box the little white dress that she dressed me in and the church bulletin that announced my baptism. I knew my godparents, although I had never had a spiritual God-centered talk with either one. Why is my baptism important? I wondered. I was an infant. Again, it was not something that I chose, but rather it was an imposed symbol of my family's culture and heritage. Ken told me that while baptism is not regenerative, it marks those within the covenant of God's family. He told me to go home and think about my baptism and about God having orchestrated my life such that I was placed in a family that raised me with religious education. I attended Catholic schools and public schools and received four Catholic sacraments, none of which I understood. Ken instructed me to go home and think about the meaning of my baptism and my history of religious instruction.

What an odd assignment, I thought!

I went home that night and I prayed that God would help me make sense of Ken's questions and of my strange feelings.

I often think about how Ken handled my questions—this one in particular. He, of course, could have cut this conversation short. When I confessed my spiritual struggle, he could have recited Acts 16:31: "Believe in the Lord Jesus and you will be saved, you and your household." Many evangelical pastors would have acted like a shark in the water smelling fresh blood at the opportunity to quote this Bible verse to someone like me! Surely it would have been an easier conversation had he handled my question by quoting the Bible. But Ken told me recently that the Holy Spirit did not give him liberty to say this. Ken felt that I needed to search my heart, and he also felt that he needed to know more about what my own religious background and training was. Ken responded to my question by making me take stock of myself before God.

I decided that my baptism meant something—although what, I wasn't sure! I decided that God's providence to provide me with more religious education than most people receive also meant something, although each jot and tittle I had to relearn. I decided that God was bigger than my consciousness.

The following Sunday, I started to go to the RP church—and not for research. That morning—February 14, 1999—I emerged from the bed of my lesbian lover and an hour later was sitting in a pew at the Syracuse RP Church. I share this detail with you not to be lurid but merely to make the point that you never know the terrain someone else has walked to come worship the Lord.

Even though I felt like a freak in that church, I was drawn to keep going back. After a subsequent meeting with Ken, I came home and my lesbian partner told me that I was changing and that she was concerned. What did I need? Some time away from my work? Maybe we needed to take that long vacation. T is a psychologist, and you can't hide a lot from a psychologist.

My transgendered friend's words were still weighing heavily upon my heart. Who is this Jesus that he heals some but not others? Is it right to pray for healing when, from the Bible's perspective, I was to repent from my sin? Does God hear prayers that are not construed in the terms he lays out in the Bible? If Jesus is the living word, can we pray "through" him if we do not follow him as our Savior and Lord? These questions weighed hard on me.

That night, I prayed, and asked God if the gospel message was for someone like me, too. I viscerally felt the living presence of God as I prayed. Jesus seemed present and alive. I knew that I was not alone in my room. I prayed that if Jesus was truly a real and risen God, that he would change my heart. And if he was real and if I was his, I prayed that he would give me the strength of mind to follow him and the character to become a godly woman. I prayed for the strength of character to repent for a sin that at that time didn't feel like sin at all—it felt like life, plain and simple. I prayed that if my life was actually his life, that he would take it back and make it what he wanted it to be. I asked him to take it all: my sexuality, my profession, my community, my tastes, my books, and my tomorrows.

Two incommensurable worldviews clashed: the reality of my lived experience and the truth of the word of God. In continental philosophy, we talk about the difference between the true and the real. Had my life become real, but not true? The Bible told me to repent, but I didn't feel like repenting. Do you have to feel like repenting in order to repent? Was I a sinner, or was I, in my drag queen friend's words, sick? How do you repent for a sin that doesn't feel like a sin? How could the thing that I had studied and become be sinful? How could I be tenured in a field that is sin? How could I and everyone that I knew and loved be in sin?

In this crucible of confusion, I learned something important. I learned the first rule of repentance: that repentance requires greater intimacy with God than with our sin. How much greater?

About the size of a mustard seed. Repentance requires that we draw near to Jesus, no matter what. And sometimes we all have to crawl there on our hands and knees. Repentance is an intimate affair. And for many of us, intimacy with anything is a terrifying prospect.

When Christ gave me the strength to follow him, I didn't stop feeling like a lesbian. I've discovered that the Lord doesn't change my feelings until I obey him. During one sermon, Ken pointed to John 7:17, and called this "the hermeneutics of obedience." Jesus is speaking in this passage, and he says: "If anyone is willing to do God's will, he will know of the teaching, whether it is of God or whether I speak from myself." Ah ha! Here it was! Obedience comes before understanding. I *wanted* to understand. But did I actually will to do his will? God promised to reveal this understanding to me if I "willed to do his will." The Bible doesn't just say *do* his will, but "will to do his will." Wanting to understand is a theoretical statement; willing to do his will takes action.

I knew I didn't have that! I prayed that the Lord would give me that wholehearted will. I learned that the Lord wants all of our loyalties under submission to him. He wants us to identify ourselves, to call ourselves by name, in his name for us. In my case, my feelings of lesbianism were familiar, comfortable, and recognizable, and I was reluctant to give them up. I clung to Matthew 16:24, remembering that every believer had to at some point in life take the step that I was taking: giving up the right to myself, taking up his Cross (i.e., the historicity of the resurrection, not masochism endured to please others), and following Jesus. The Lord made it clear to me that I had to make some serious life changes.

I started to obey God in my heart one step at a time. I broke up with my girlfriend. My heart really wasn't in the breakup, but I hoped that God would regard my obedience even in its double-mindedness. I started to go to the RP church fully, in my heart, for the whole purpose of worshiping God. I stopped caring if I looked like a freak there. I started to receive the friendship that the church members offered to me. I learned that we must obey in faith before we feel better or different. At this time, though, obeying in faith, to me, felt like throwing myself off a cliff. Faith that endures is heroic, not sentimental.

And then came the night terrors. Night after night, dreams so vivid and real that I could taste and feel them. Dreams so commanding that when I finally awoke, I felt filthy and delirious.

My journey out of lesbianism was messy and difficult. I spent a lot of time in prayer—and still do. I leaned heavily on the counsel of the women of the Syracuse church: Floy Smith, Vivian Rice, NM, Becky Smith, Robyn Zorn, Corrine Thompson, Marty Wright, Kathy Donath. I asked them vulnerable and real questions and they answered me and loved me anyway. The journey out of lesbianism had many dimensions, and the Lord was gracious in leading me a small step, and then burning the bridge I crossed to keep me safely closer to him. From the first night, there was no going back.

Slowly but steadily, my feelings did start to change—feelings about myself as a woman and feelings about what sexuality really is and what it really isn't. I—like most everyone who identified as gay or lesbian—felt very comfortable, very at home in my body, in my lesbianism. One doesn't repent for a sin of identity in one session. Sins of identity have multiple dimensions, and throughout this journey, I have come to my pastor and his wife, friends in the Lord, and always to the Lord himself with different facets of my sin. I don't mean different incidents or examples of the same sin, but different facets of sin—how pride, for example, informed my decision-making, or how my unwillingness to forgive others had landlocked my heart in bitterness. I have walked this journey with help. There is no other way to do it. I still walk this journey with help.

The teaching, the prayers, and the friendships the Lord has given to me through the Body of Christ have blessed me richly. I'm grateful that the Lord brought me to a church that was as strong on teaching as it is on compassion. Did I find the perfect church? No. I almost left when things got hard, and they got hard fast. The time that I brought my drag queen friend to church pushed a lot of folks out of their comfort zone.

When a lesbian student of mine recovered from a suicide attempt first at the pastor's home and then later at my home, and the Christian community and the lesbian community had to spend a lot of time together, I was really nervous. My lesbian friends had to learn that not all Christians are bigots. My Christian friends had to learn that Christians have a lot to learn from gay and lesbian folks about mercy work. At first, I missed the power in this fruitful exchange, and instead felt deeply uncomfortable. I didn't know how to bridge the two groups.

Sharing this one Friday night at the home of Ron and Robyn Zorn, Ron reminded me that bridges get walked on and that is a normal part of being a bridge. Ah ha! And then I relaxed, remembering that this is the Lord's work, not mine. Bridges, though, do get walked on, and if the Lord calls us to be a bridge, we have to learn to bear in his strength the weight. And it hurts. And it's good. And the Lord equips. As he promises in Scripture, he gives us the strength that we need to stand steadfast and trust in him. The Syracuse church no doubt grew in compassion because of the urgency of need that I brought, and my lesbian community grew in knowledge of what life in Christ can look like.

God sent me to a Reformed and Presbyterian conservative church to repent, heal, learn, and thrive. The pastor there did not farm me out to a para-church ministry "specializing" in "gay people." He and the session knew that the church is competent to counsel (to quote the title of one of Jay Adams's useful books). I needed (and need) faithful shepherding, not the glitz and glamor that has captured the soul of modern evangelical culture. I had to lean and lean hard on the full weight of Scripture, on the fullness of the word of God, and I'm grateful that when I heard the Lord's call on my life, and I wanted to hedge my bets, keep my girlfriend, and add a little God to my life, I had a pastor and friends in the Lord who asked nothing less of me than that I die to myself. Biblical orthodoxy can offer real compassion, because in our struggle against sin we cannot undermine God's power to change lives.

Healing comes through God's work, and God deals differently with us when we deal differently with him. When we repent, he hears. Do I believe that I'm healed? Yes. My life shows the signs. My life went from black-and-white to color. At first I didn't recognize myself in the world. Today, I don't recognize myself in the pictures from my life as a lesbian.

Dr. Maureen Vanterpool, a colleague from Geneva College, told me recently that being a lesbian was a case of mistaken identity. This became an intriguing and important paradigm for me. And even though I'm no longer a lesbian, I'm still a sinner.

I'm redeemed, but still fallen. And sin is sin. I believe that the Lord is more grieved by the sins of my current life than by my past life as a lesbian. How did the Lord heal me? The way that he always heals: the word of God got to be bigger inside me than I. My natural inclination was to resist, so like a reflex, I did this. God's people surrounded me. Not to manipulate. Not to badger. But to love and to listen and to watch and to pray. And eventually instead of resisting, I surrendered.

Shortly after becoming a Christian, I counseled a woman who was in a closeted lesbian relationship and a member of a Bible-believing church. No one in her church knew. Therefore, no one in her church was praying for her. Therefore, she sought and received no counsel. There was no "bearing one with the other" for her. No confession. No repentance. No healing. No joy in Christ. Just isolation. And shame. And pretense. Someone had sold her the pack of lies that said that God can heal your lying tongue or your broken heart, even cure your cancer if he chooses, but he can't transform your sexuality. I told her that my heart breaks for her isolation and shame and asked her why she didn't share her struggle with anyone in her church. She said: "Rosaria, if people in my church really believed that gay people could be transformed by Christ, they wouldn't talk about us or pray about us in the hateful way that they do."

Christian reader, is this what people say about you when they hear you talk and pray? Do your prayers rise no higher than your prejudice?

I think that churches would be places of greater intimacy and growth in Christ if people stopped lying about what we need, what we fear, where we fail, and how we sin. I think that many of us have a hard time believing the God we believe in, when the going gets tough. And I suspect that, instead of seeking counsel and direction from those stronger in the Lord, we retreat into our isolation and shame and let the sin wash over us, defeating us again. Or maybe we muscle through on our pride. Do we really believe that the word of God is a double-edged sword, cutting between the spirit and the soul? Or do we use the word of God as a cue card to commandeer only our external behavior?

Although grateful, I did not perceive conversion to be "a blessing." It was a train wreck. After we profess faith in Christ, the next morning, the alarm still rings and we have to swing our feet out of bed and do something. And, while we cannot lose our salvation, if we are not growing in spiritual maturity we can lose everything else. What I faced at work following my conversion was the rubbish of my sin, forgiven by God, but still there to be cleared away. This required a newer and even more intense understanding and application of Scripture.

When I became a Christian, I had to change everything—my life, my friends, my writing, my teaching, my advising, my clothes, my speech, my thoughts. I was tenured to a field that I could no longer work in. I was the faculty advisor to all of the gay and lesbian and feminist groups on campus. I was writing a book that I no longer believed in. And, I was scheduled in a few months to give the incoming address to all of Syracuse University's graduate students. What in the world would I say to them? The lecture that I had written and planned to deliver—on Queer Theory—I threw in the trash. Thousands of new students would hear my first, fledgling attempts to speak about Christian hermeneutics at a postmodern university. I was flooded with doubt about my new life in Christ. Was I willing to suffer like Christ? Was I willing to be considered stupid by those who didn't know Jesus? The world's eyes register what a life in Christ takes away, but how do I communicate all that it gives? Do I really believe, in Charles Bridges's words, "The very chains of Christ are glorious" (p. 33)?[1] Peter, after being beaten for preaching the gospel, rejoiced that he was "counted worthy to suffer shame for [Christ's] name" (Acts 5:41). I pondered this. To the world, this is masochism. To the Christian, this is freedom. Did I really believe this? Do I really believe this today?

I wondered: If my life was the only evidence that Christ was alive, would anyone be convinced?

And what about my home, my *habitus*? A habitus is a way of life that forms habits of the head, habits of the heart, and habits of the mind. My habitus had heretofore been a bastion of leftist political activism. What does a Christian habitus look like, especially one run by a single ex-lesbian with a now-defunct PhD?

And what about my drag queen friend, who had prayed for the Lord's healing? What exactly did that mean? What exactly is repentance? If it is a way of life for a Christian, I needed to understand it fully, comprehensively, deeply, and well.

And what of my responsibilities to my gay friends? Were their secrets still safe with me?

What does joy in Christ mean when faced with duties that you don't want?

As I am sure is clear by these concerns, I did not, in any way, want to "share the hope that lies within me." I wanted to go back to bed and draw the covers over my head.

Conversion put me in a complicated and comprehensive chaos. I sometimes wonder, when I hear other Christians pray for the salvation of the "lost," if they realize that this comprehensive chaos is the desired end of such prayers. Often, people asked me to describe the lessons I learned from this experience. I can't. It was too traumatic. Sometimes in crisis, we don't really learn lessons. Sometimes the result is simpler and more profound: sometimes our character is simply transformed.

Repentance and the Sin of Sodom

Syracuse, N.Y., April 1999–August 2000

In April 1999, I felt the call of Jesus Christ upon my life. It was both subtle and blatant, like the peace inside the eye of the hurricane. I could in no way resist and I in no way understood what would become of my life. I know, I know. How do I know it was Jesus? Maybe it was my Catholic guilt, my caffeine-driven subconscious, or last night's curry tofu. Well, I don't. But I believed—and believe—that it was Jesus.

At this time, I was just starting to pray that God would show me my sins and help me to repent of them. I didn't understand why homosexuality was a sin, why something in the particular manifestation of same-gender love was wrong in itself. But I did know that pride was a sin, and so I decided to start there. As I began to pray and repent, I wondered: could pride be the root of all my sins? I wondered: what was the real sin of Sodom? I had always thought that God's judgment upon Sodom (in Genesis 19) clearly singled out and targeted homosexuality. I believed that God's judgment against Sodom exemplified the fiercest of God's judgments. But as I read more deeply in the Bible, I ran across a passage that made me stop and think. This passage in the book of Ezekiel revealed to me that Sodom was indicted for materialism and neglect of the poor and needy—and, that homosexuality was a symptom and an extension of these other sins. In this passage, God is speaking to his chosen people in Jerusalem and warning them about their hidden sin, using Sodom as an example.

Importantly, God does not say that this sin of Sodom is the worst of all sins. Instead, God uses the sin of Sodom to reveal the greater sin committed by his own people:

> "As I live," says the Lord God, "neither your sister Sodom nor her daughters have done as you and your daughters have done. Look, this was the iniquity of your sister Sodom: She and her daughters had pride, fullness of food, and abundance of idleness; neither did she strengthen the hand of the poor and needy. And they were haughty and committed abomination before Me; therefore I took them away as I saw fit." (Ezek. 16:48-50)

I found this passage to reveal some surprising things. In it, God is comparing Jerusalem to Sodom and saying that Sodom's sin is less offensive to God than Jerusalem's. Next, God tells us what is at the root of homosexuality and what the progression of sin is. We read here that the root of homosexuality is also the root of a myriad of other sins. First, we find pride ("[Sodom] and her daughters had pride"). Why pride? Pride is the root of all sin. Pride puffs one up with a false sense of independence. Proud people always feel that they can live independently from God and from other people. Proud people feel entitled to do what they want when they want to.

Second, we find wealth ("fullness of food") and an entertainment-driven worldview ("abundance of idleness"). Living according to God's standards is an acquired taste. We develop a taste for godly living only by intentionally putting into place practices that equip us to live below our means. We develop a taste for God's standards only by disciplining our minds, hands, money, and time. In God's economy, what we love we will discipline. God did not create us so that we would, as the title of an early book on postmodernism declares, "amuse ourselves to death." Undisciplined taste will always lead to egregious sin—slowly and almost imperceptibly.

Third, we find lack of mercy ("neither did she strengthen the hand of the poor and needy"). Refusing to be the merciful neighbor in the extreme terms exemplified by the Samaritan traveler to his cultural enemy left to die on the road to Jericho

(Luke 10:25-37) leads to egregious sin. I think this is a shocking truth and I imagine that most Bible-believing Christians would be horrified to see this truth exposed in such bare terms! God calls us to be merciful to others *for our own good* as well as for the good of our community. Our hearts will become hard to the whispers of God if we turn our backs on those who have less than we do.

Fourth, we find lack of discretion and modesty ("they were haughty and committed abomination before Me"). Pride combined with wealth leads to idleness because you falsely feel that God just wants you to have fun; if unchecked, this sin will grow into entertainment-driven lust; if unchecked, this sin will grow into hardness of heart that declares other people's problems no responsibility or care of your own; if unchecked, we become bold in our sin and feel entitled to live selfish lives fueled by the twin values of our culture: acquiring and achieving. Modesty and discretion are not old-fashioned values. They are God's standards that help us to encourage one another in good works, not covetousness.

You might notice that there is nothing inherently sexual about any of these sins: pride, wealth, entertainment-driven focus, lack of mercy, lack of modesty. We like to think that sin is contained by categories of logic or psychology. It's not. So why do we assume that sexual sin has sexual or affectual origins? That is because we have too narrow a focus about sexuality's purview. Sexuality isn't about what we do in bed. Sexuality encompasses a whole range of needs, demands, and desires. Sexuality is more a symptom of our life's condition than a cause, more a consequence than an origin.

Importantly, we don't see God making fun of homosexuality or regarding it as a different, unusual, or exotic sin. What we see instead is God's warning: If you indulge the sins of pride, wealth, entertainment-lust, lack of mercy, and lack of discretion, you will find yourself deep in sin—and the type of sin may surprise you. That sin may attach itself to a pattern of life closely or loosely linked to this list. While sin is not contained by logical categories of progression, nonetheless, sin *is* progressive. That is, while sin does not stay contained by type or trope, if ignored, excused, or enjoyed, sin grows and spreads like poison ivy.

But God is a God of mercy, redemption, second chances, and salvation. And therefore, when Jesus uses Sodom as an example during his ministry on earth, the example reveals that God is angrier at the religious people of Jesus' day than the inhabitants of Sodom. Jesus says this to God's people in Capernaum:

> And you, Capernaum, who are exalted to heaven, will be brought to Hades; for if the mighty works which were done in you had been done in Sodom, it would have remained until this day. But I say to you that it shall be more tolerable for the land of Sodom in the day of judgment than for you. (Matt. 11:23-24)

Jesus tells us clearly that had Sodom seen God's power manifested before them as Capernaum had, they would have repented and lived. Jesus' injunction that God is more greatly grieved by the sins of those who claim to know him than by those who know him not, struck a chord for me. There is a fairness and capaciousness to Jesus' words that simply is not reflected in modern evangelical culture. We see this capaciousness reflected in Jesus' invitation noted in the chapter's end. Jesus declares: "Come to Me, all you who labor and are heavy laden, and I will give you rest. Take My yoke upon you and learn from Me, for I am gentle and lowly in heart, and you will find rest for your souls. For My yoke is easy and My burden is light" (Matt. 11:28-30). These passages also convicted me that homosexuality—like all sin—is symptomatic and not causal—that is, it tells us where our heart has been, not who we inherently are or what we are destined to become.*

These passages forced me to see pride and not sexual orientation as the root sin. In turn, this shaped the way that I reflected on my whole life, in the context of the word of God. I realized that my sexuality had never been pure and my relationships never honored the other person or the Lord. My moral code encompassed serial monogamy, "safe" sex, and sex only in the context of love. Love, grounded only in personal feelings as mine had been, changes without warning or logic. The truth is, outside of Christ, I am a manipulator, liar, power-monger, and controller. In my

---

* My husband, Kent, has given me, over the years, a deeper appreciation of this passage and its pivotal role in understanding the social nature and emotional root of sexual sin. I am indebted to his sensitivity about this; my own healing continues to build as I drink deeply of the radical implications of biblical sexuality, and as repentance chips away at me from the inside out.

relationships with men and with women, I had to be in charge. I killed with kindness and slayed with gifts. I bought people's loyalties and affections. I had been a lesbian for almost a decade. I considered myself an "informed" lesbian—someone who had had relationships with men and found them wanting and dissatisfying. I did not consider myself bisexual because I had had no intention of having a relationship with a man ever again. I did not find men compelling or interesting. My lesbian identity began in nonsexual ways: I have always enjoyed the good communication that women share. I also found myself bonding with women over shared hobbies and interests and feminist and leftist political values. I'm not given to pornography in any form, and therefore visual attraction never motivated my friendships or responses to other people. I share my sexual history with you not to flaunt my sin or offend my reader, but to reveal that my sexuality was sinful not because it was lesbian *per se* but because it wasn't Christ-controlled. My heterosexual past was no more sanctified than my homosexual present. God had revealed that to me powerfully as I sat under the preaching of his word, as I read the Bible, and as I talked to other Christians in my church about what sexuality meant in God's economy. In understanding myself as a sexual being, responding to Jesus (i.e., "committing my life to Christ") meant not going backwards to my heterosexual past but going forward to something entirely new. At the time I thought that this would most likely be celibacy and the single life. Sexuality that did not devour the other person seemed unimaginable to me. And while I never really liked the idea of growing old alone, I accepted that if God could take me this far in life safely, he would see me through this next part, too.

Every aspect of my life came under the scrutiny of my new Christian worldview. It was like someone turned the search light on and I couldn't dim the intensity. I understood why the Pharisee Saul on the road to Damascus was struck blind for three days from the light of the gospel! I learned that sin roots not in outward behaviors, but in patterns of thinking. I felt like a non-native speaker as I fumbled around as a new Christian. My housemate (not my ex-lover but someone who rented a room in my house) was a lesbian writer and Wiccan witch who had recently undergone a messy breakup. She wanted to know if she had to move out—now that I was a Christian and all. We had a long talk about tolerance and honesty. She was a gentle spirit and had helped me to find balance before, and I was glad that she wasn't going to move out right away. We decided she should stay for the summer and planned for a November 1999 move-out date. We settled into our domestic routine.

As I reread my life, I realized that my sexual sin was rooted not only in pride but also in a false understanding about gender. I came to the understanding that I could not possibly be a godly woman if I didn't even know how to be a *woman*. Pastor Ken preached a sermon that really brought this point home to me, and one Monday afternoon, after praying fervently for God to show me how to live as a godly woman, I went through the church directory and picked out the three women whose godliness, sense of self, personal strength, and integrity really stood out to me. I picked women who were different from me, but people who would answer me honestly. I called Becky Smith, Corrine Thompson, and Kathy Donath. I asked simple questions, even perhaps naive ones, and I remember how tender each woman was in answering my questions. I was still struggling with my identity, now with my new Christian identity. How could a woman "like me" be a godly woman? Each woman directed me to Mary Magdalene and to the Proverbs 31 woman. Each woman reminded me that knowing God's forgiveness in a real and vital way is the root of all godliness—for men or for women.

Making a life commitment to Christ was not merely a philosophical shift. It was not a one-step process. It did not involve rearranging the surface prejudices and fickle loyalties of my life. Conversion didn't "fit" my life. Conversion overhauled my soul and personality. It was arduous and intense. I experienced with great depth the power and authority of God in my life. In it I learned—and am still learning—how to love God with all my heart, soul, strength, and mind. When you die to yourself, you have nothing from your past to use as clay out of which to shape your future.

Because conversion, in Scripture and in my personal experience, is arduous and transformative, I fear the consequence of the easy believism that typifies modern evangelical culture. I live now in a neighborhood that often seems like the Disneyland of evangelical culture. I have neighbors who are members of one of the big churches in our community. Their church has a fast-food restaurant (so no one gets hungry), a well-known coffee chain (so no one gets sleepy or feels deprived of creature comforts), and a Moon bounce (so children will think that God just wants you to have fun). The church organizes a church-sponsored pool (i.e., gambling program) around the NCAA Final Four.

When we compare what we do at church, what we learn in Bible study, and what we mean when we call ourselves followers of Christ, our vocabulary may be the same, but the meaning behind our vocabulary is vastly different. And when it comes down to how we parent our children, the differences are profound. Another church in our neighborhood is projecting a budget of 19 million dollars to build their Tabernacle, following this same model. These churches define themselves as purpose-driven and seeker-friendly. And their annual budgets, as missionary friends pointed out to me, could feed all the AIDS orphans in Africa for years. Just their Sunday morning doughnut budget would make a big dent in the problem of Third World poverty!

The purpose-driven movement makes conversion a simple matter of saying the magic words, a mantra that makes Jesus the Mister Rogers of the conscience. In his popular book, *The Purpose Driven Life*,[2] author Rick Warren represents conversion in these words: "Jesus, I believe in you and I receive you" (p. 59). There is a pit of false hope in placing our faith in our words rather than in God's compassion to receive sinners to himself. Warren falsely (and dangerously) assures us of our salvation. He writes: "If you sincerely meant that prayer, congratulations! Welcome to the family of God!" (p. 59). How do I judge my own sincerity? The saving grace of salvation is located in a holy and electing God, and a sacrificing, suffering, and obedient Savior. Stakes this high can never rest on my sincerity.

When I read something like this, I do not recognize Jesus, the Holy Bible, my conversion or myself at all. Recently, on vacation in South Carolina, my husband and I went to a "community church." My conservative Reformed Presbyterian pastor and husband noted when we got back to the hotel room that we had just witnessed a service that contained a baptism without water, preaching without Scripture, conversation about disappointment and pithy observations about financial responsibility without prayer, the distribution of flowers and trinkets without grace, and a dismissal without a blessing. Everyone was smiling, though, when it came time to walk out the door. This church's conversion prayer was printed in the bulletin. It read like this: "Dear God, I'm so sorry for my mistakes. Thanks for salvation."

These misrepresentations of the gospel are dangerous and misleading. Sin is not a mistake. A mistake is taking the wrong exit on the highway. A sin is treason against a Holy God. A mistake is a logical misstep. Sin lurks in our heart and grabs us by the throat to do its bidding. Remember what God said to Cain about his sin? It's true for us too. In the fourth chapter of Genesis, God warns Cain like this: "Sin lies at the door. And its desire is for you, but you should rule over it" (Gen. 4:6). In accepting misrepresentations of the gospel that render sin anything less than this, you will never learn of the fruit of repentance. The Apostle Paul defines his post-conversion life simply: in Christ he now does "works befitting repentance" (Acts 26:20). This idea that we repent and we serve is also reflected in the words of the last of the Old Testament prophets, John the Baptist, who prepares the way of the Lord by warning the religious people of his day to "Repent, for the kingdom of God is at hand!" (Matt. 3:2) and, after repenting, to "bear fruits worthy of repentance" (Matt. 3:8). And Jesus himself warns us against failing to count the costs of discipleship or of testing ourselves in the faith, when he says,

> "Not everyone who says to Me, 'Lord, Lord,' shall enter the kingdom of heaven, but he who does the will of My Father in heaven. Many will say to me in that day, 'Lord, Lord, have we not prophesied in Your name, cast out demons in Your name, and done many wonders in Your name?' And then I will declare to them, 'I never knew you; depart from Me, you who practice lawlessness.'" (Matt. 7:21-23)

The Christian life is a life imbued with the supernatural power and authority of God. God is the God of salvation. We do not control God by saying magic words or attending church. Conversion is a heart-affair. Before we can come to Christ, we must empty ourselves of the false pride, blame-shifting, excuse-making, and self-deception that preoccupy our days and our relationships. Before we can come to Christ, we must come to ourselves.

After conversion, every day and every part of the routine of my life was a faith test. I had formerly been a very popular teacher in gay and lesbian studies. I was already scheduled to teach for the fall semester 1999 Introduction to Women's Studies (a class that routinely enrolled over 200 students) and Feminist Pedagogy (a graduate seminar for graduate students who taught under me). I would have to follow through and teach these classes, but would have to find a way to teach them as a Christian. I still needed to make course descriptions for the classes in Christian hermeneutics that I would teach for the spring semester 2000. I had liberty to teach new courses—as long as the classes drew students. I had formerly used my classroom to advocate for gay and lesbian rights and ideas. I now used my classroom to abandon the discipline in which I was hired to create instead courses in a field of study—Christian hermeneutics—unheard of in my liberal postmodern department. Who would take such courses? What if no one signed up?

Each day brought a deluge of moral choices couched in the daily routine of a radical professor. Each day, R was there to support me through these. He would tell me to be like King David, the Prophet Daniel, and the Apostle Paul. He also shared with me the details of his daily struggle with sexual sin, and in so doing made me feel less alone in my own journey. But by the time the summer ended, I noticed something: God was healing me. I was repenting and God was healing me. At the same time, R seemed stuck in the same place. I prayed daily for him. I wondered why he was not experiencing any liberty from his sin, as I was experiencing from mine.

I also started to notice something else about my life: I wasn't plagued with anxiety or nightmares anymore. The intestinal distress that had been my daily companion was no longer a part of my life (and I hadn't taken a Tums in months). I changed my exercise routine from intense running to active walking. I cleaned my house and my office the way God was cleaning my soul: I pitched things that weren't honoring to God. I got rid of whole libraries of books,

CDs, movies, pictures. I unsubscribed to magazines and professional journals. I suddenly had time in my life to reflect. I took up gardening. I enjoyed baking bread from scratch for my friends and neighbors. I relaxed. I grew in strength in the Lord. I forgave my enemies and enjoyed the solitude of daily prayer. I read and reread the Bible, searching for examples for my life. Jesus was my Teacher and the Apostle Paul my brother and kindred spirit. I started to develop real friendships from within my church family.

During one of my weekly discipleship meetings with Floy, she asked me if I had thought about church membership. Church membership? Me? *This* church? I was horrified! Membership! Yuck! I have never been a person given to joining clubs and I found the whole question to be antithetical to my free spirit. I told Floy that I loved our church but that I didn't see any reason to "join the club." She then told me something that really made me stop and think: She said that every believer in the Bible is what we would consider today to be a church member. There is no such thing as an independent Christian. At the 2004 Reformed Presbyterian International Conference, I heard Pastor Ted Donnelly put it this way. Imagine, he said, if the U.S. declared that we were going to send one soldier to Iraq. One soldier! Even with the best equipment in the world, how could one little soldier survive? His point resonated with me and reminded me of Floy's counsel about church membership: Nobody goes into battle alone. Sanctification—growing in Christ—is always both personal and communal. We need one another. Our faith struggles and our successes are part of the Body of Christ, not possessed by our own little kingdom. This Christian life was war—of this I was certain. Who in her right mind, Floy asked, would go to war without an army?

The covenant membership vows of the Reformed Presbyterian Church are simple, yet they cut me to the core. Here are our seven vows of church membership. After each vow, I have recorded my initial internal turmoil:

Official Vows: Covenant of Church Membership

1. *Do you believe the Scriptures of the Old and New Testaments to be the word of God, the only infallible rule of faith and life?*

My "rule of faith and life" had been my own intellect. As a document wholly produced through oral history, I had had no faith in the Bible as true or accurate. Indeed, as a scholar, I wouldn't even have trusted a chocolate chip cookie recipe passed down through oral history, and here I was putting my life on the line—for a document produced by something as intellectually flimsy as oral history! Only the seriously anti-intellectual would do this. And what about the ontological fallacy inherent in using the Bible to "prop up" God while simultaneously using God to "prop up" the Bible? How could a committed postmodernist like me believe that the gospel is true?

2. Do you believe in the one living and true God—the Father, Son and Holy Spirit, as revealed in the Scriptures?
I had believed that God was an imperialist social construct invented to soothe the consciousness of the intellectually infirm. Friedrich Nietzsche was kinder than I in his assessment that God is dead.

3. Do you repent of your sin; confess your guilt and helplessness as a sinner against God; profess Jesus Christ, Son of God, as your Saviour and Lord; and dedicate yourself to His service: Do you promise that you will endeavor to forsake all sin, and to conform your life to His teaching and example?
Repent? Sin? Guilt? Helplessness? These were once anathema to my character and life. After all, I had given speeches to gathering crowds at gay pride marches! Profess Jesus Christ as my Savior and Lord? The very name of Jesus I had once hated—deeply—and the only time his name was uttered from my mouth was in cursing something.

4. Do you promise to submit in the Lord to the teaching and government of this church as being based upon the Scriptures and described in substance in the Constitution of the Reformed Presbyterian Church of North America? *Do you recognize your responsibility to work with others in the church and do you promise to support and encourage them in their service to the Lord? In case you should need correction in doctrine or life, do you promise to respect the authority and discipline of the church?*

Submit myself to the elders of my church? Submit myself to a bunch of men, not one of whom had a PhD? Had I lost my mind? What would this look like? Would they come to my Women's Studies 101 lectures and hold up placards at the end of each lecture, taunting my double-mindedness and disloyalty?

5. To the end that you may grow in the Christian life, do you promise that you will diligently read the Bible, engage in private prayer, keep the Lord's Day, regularly attend the worship services, observe the appointed sacraments, and give to the Lord's work as He shall prosper you?

How will I build my empire if I spend all of this time on God? How will I conduct my professional life without using Sunday as a workday?

6. Do you purpose to seek first the kingdom of God and His righteousness in all the relationships of life, faithfully to perform your whole duty as a true servant of Jesus Christ, and seek to win others to Him?

I had always sought first the kingdom of my own pleasure and person. I sought to win others to myself and myself alone.

7. Do you make this profession of faith and purpose in the presence of God, in humble reliance upon His grace, as you desire to give your account with joy at the Last Great Day?

I didn't like thinking about my mortality or about the Last Great Day. I had buried countless gay friends to the AIDS epidemic, and it felt blasphemous to even entertain the idea that, after a hellish death, they would now spend eternity in hell. I almost feared that believing this condemned them to hell.

In July 1999, I made my profession of faith before God, before the elders of my church at one meeting and before my church congregation during a worship service. Ken Smith had taught me that I was not "joining" a church, but rather, was making a covenant with God and with a church body. As I stood before the congregation to make this profession of faith, I felt the assault of my disloyalty to the gay community as powerfully as I did my loyalty to Christ. Indeed, I could barely speak the "I do." Pastor Ken took my uncontrolled shaking as consent and the rest of the congregation took me on faith. I still remember the trauma in my body when I hear our membership vows or watch someone stand before the congregation for the purpose of baptism or church membership. Each Lord's Supper made me experience my traitorship to my gay friends and to the person that I once was.

It took me three months after committing my life to Christ to consent to these vows because I was afraid to move too far away from my life, as I had known it. A chapter of my life had just closed, but I had no idea at the time how severely I would feel its closure. Consenting to these vows meant simply that there was no going back. Once I had said these vows with my lips and held them in my heart, therein truly lay my treason from the gay community. I felt like I lived in some liminal invisible place, with no history and no sense of future. I felt like a vampire—possessing no reflection in mirrors. I realize now that this is what it means to be washed clean, to be truly made new again. The past really is gone. The shadow of what was remains, but the substance is truly taken away. The Apostle Paul explains it this way, "I do not count myself to have apprehended, but one thing I do, forgetting those things which are behind and reaching forward to those things which are ahead" (Phil. 3:13). This forgetting was a painful process. Like grief, the cost of relief is the *you* that you used to be. Surviving means sacrificing something of you.

On August 17, 1999, I returned to my office after delivering a lecture to all incoming graduate students. The topic was to be of my choosing. When the graduate school invited me, I was a lesbian postmodernist. When I delivered the lecture six months later, I was a fledgling follower of Jesus Christ. The lecture was entitled: "The Solomon Problem." I felt awkward and uncomfortable as I took the podium and adjusted the clip-on microphone to the neckline of my dress. I was in process of growing out my butch haircut, so every day was a bad hair day. And the lecture was going to be a bomb. In it, I would become a traitor and a turncoat. To the lesbian community, I would become the example of what not to be. I could not have gotten through that lecture had R not been there. In the six months since my conversion, he had become my watchdog, big brother, champion, simultaneous translator, and best friend. He came to my lectures, to my classes, to my Thursday night dinners. He talked to my students and my colleagues. He embraced my drag queen friends. He translated my concerns to the session of our church with a deftness and sensitivity that I still marvel at. As I fingered my pages on the podium, R gave me a firm thumbs up from his spot, the nosebleed section of the balcony, and left of stage. He was the only person who understood this spiritual and professional schizophrenia that had quickly become my new normal after conversion. Here is the talk that I gave that day:

What King Solomon Teaches Those in the Wisdom Business: Active Learning and Active Scholarship

Since I was 16 years old, I have been inspired by three categories of ideas: text—the written testimony of experience and meaning; history—the content of events that stands outside of consciousness and shapes it perpetually; and mercy—the category of selfless love and stealth compassion. These categories have never been merely academic, and indeed, they have saved my life on more than one occasion. As a child and teenager, I used these categories to store understanding about the dynamics in my home. I wrote my first book about this. As an adult, these categories have expanded to address the historicity of social genocide to the historicity of the resurrection; the authority of texts produced in the social margins of women's literature to the Bible as an authoritative text, the written revelation of the living triune God (too often misread and misused as our contemporary political Trojan horse); from social justice on behalf of women, people of color, the disabled, and queer liberation to the counterintuitive lessons of mercy taught in the New Testament. Text, History, and Mercy. These categories raise my life's Big Questions. What are yours? What are yours?

This leads me to my first point about real learning: It's not a recipe, it's not a toolbox that neatly fashions any notion, no matter how bankrupt or dubious or silly. At least two decades of poststructural and postmodern research have equipped intellectuals with powerful methods to question the reliability of truth-claims and procedures of evidence, and to reveal the social effects of oppression produced by epistemological imperialism. But the powerful legacy poststructuralism bequeaths to contemporary intellectuals should not create its own hegemony of intellectual expectation, one which categorically trades in truth for doubt and faith for skepticism. Students smell fear, laziness, and fraudulence faster than a scavenger on road kill, and real learning depends on our quest for real knowledge, not its perpetual deferment in the form of endless doubt. In order to seek real knowledge, we will confront times when we have to choose between the old ideas that give us comfort in their familiarity or the safe paradigms that encourage endless questioning for the bold quest of capacious truth. Knowledge depends on the renewal of our minds. If you fear such renewal and its consequences, then you don't belong in graduate school. This may seem like a tall order, perhaps even an unfriendly one, and you should get a second opinion, to be sure. From my position, though, the stakes only get higher from this day on, so risking immediate comfort and facing instead the Big Questions is a skill that must begin early if it is to begin at all.

Graduate school can be like purgatory, and at various times professors make proclamations, as I just did a sentence ago, about who belongs in graduate school and who doesn't. Professors usually base these judgments on grades, scores on comprehensive examinations, expedience in academic hoop jumping, publications, and too often for my moral code, the disciple's adoration of the mentor. For graduate students, the value of your undergraduate teaching may seem as distant as Kansas and the pursuit of deep ethical questions as unreclaimable as the sting of your first skinned knee. Here's my advice: don't buy it. Strong scholars and successful professors experience bumpy roads in graduate school and after. Learn how to fall on your face and pick yourself up. Learn how to turn the train around. Learn how to glean good lessons from bad teachers in an effort to be a good teacher to those undergraduates under your care. Learn to look up, act on faith that the Big Picture has purpose: Failing an exam does not mean that you don't belong here. The only people who don't belong in the classroom, library, laboratory, or lecturing from the podium are those who fear confrontation of incommensurable truth-claims, and who seek safety over the production and excavation of ideas—even scary ideas. If truth-claims, the scholarly evidence that supports them, and the opportunity to engage in meaningful and testy debate with those who think differently than you do are burning in your heart and mind, then you are in the right place and I have only one thing to say: welcome home.

In juxtaposing truth-claims with endless questions or in advancing the case that we make decisions based in articulated presuppositional values, I intend no formula. Newer is not always better. Nor is the traditional more solid than the contemporary. It's not that easy. The university classroom is neither a shopping mall whose existence depends on disseminating the latest, sexiest critical approach, nor a museum, where ideas are valued because of tradition alone and where you can look but never touch. Instead, the classroom is a place of joy fueled by the quest for excellence and the productive fear generated by the awesomeness of our ignorance and our inability to transform human reason into wisdom on its own terms, when it is unhinged from a living God. If you remember the Big Questions and claim them in your heart as your Big Questions, you will find that there are more ways to succeed than to fail and you will be connected to something that matters. Don't fret because your path to those Big Questions doesn't look like somebody else's journey. Don't fret when the path is lonely or treacherous. Look up.

Enjoy the classroom. Enjoy the opportunity to touch the lives of others. Cherish the sacred relationship of student to teacher. Learn how to adjust your focus. Find ways to trans-mogrify the emotional manipulation or bad manners that some of your students will no doubt display as opportunities to turn the train around. Find ways to see past the symptom of seeming boredom or disrespect to its source, and then work from that. Listen first—and listen last—and listen in between. Bring the outside into your classrooms and bring your classroom outside to bear on the world.

Think about the categories that frame your Big Questions. Write them down. Think about the life lessons that shape them. Remember who you are and the road on which you traveled to get here. I'll leave you with three of my life lessons on which I rely.

Lesson #1: *When you don't know what to do, go back to the basics.*

When I used to run marathons, I had a training partner who would say to me, at the most horrific moments, usually at about mile 20, "Rosaria, this could be the best moment of your life." I thought this man was certifiably nuts, a DSM-IV special. I tried to ignore him. But later I started to understand his meaning. This expression teaches me now that while I am motivated by the Big Questions, I do not have the Big Picture. I do not know how student resistance, classroom explosions, my own general screwing up, or mean-spirited colleagues will really affect my success or failure as an intellectual and a teacher. So I find myself, in life's most unbearable moments, in and out of the classroom, saying, "This may be the best moment of my life." At first, this makes me feel, perhaps too viscerally, that I am on mile 20 of the marathon and I'm about to throw up. And then it reminds me that even if I do throw up, I still have a marathon to finish, and something extraordinary will happen in the process of focusing on the rigor and simplicity of putting one foot in front of the next.

Lesson #2: *Speak the truth, because you never know who is listening.*

For a decade of my life, I lived as a lesbian and was a spokesperson for gay, lesbian, bisexual and transgendered issues on the local and national front. One morning, as was my routine on my way to work, I stopped at the Jordan mini-mart to get a cup of coffee. On this particular morning, I heard a woman yelling at her kids, telling them that they were worthless and inconvenient and in the way. Nothing makes me more furious than the disrespect of children, and I turned to give her my iciest glare.

That's when I saw the T-shirt she was wearing. It featured the General Mills cartoon rabbit speaking these words to an effeminate man: "Silly Faggot, Dicks are for Chicks."

There in the Jordan mini-mart on a regular day in June 1996, I decided that ideas were bigger than I was, and I approached the woman. I told her that I was a lesbian and that my feelings were hurt by her T-shirt. At first she didn't comprehend what I was saying, and so I said it again. She got it. Her jaw dropped like a fish on a line. The mini-mart went pin-dropping silent. Finally, her husband elbowed her and said, "Stop talking to the queer." I started to cry and the mini-mart exploded in laughter. When I returned to the mini-mart on the next day, stubbornness overruling fear, the woman behind the counter pulled me aside to ask me a question. It turns out that her daughter was a lesbian, and she needed help.

Lesson #3: *It's better to be wrong on an important subject than right on a trivial one, as long as you are willing to learn from your mistakes.*

This lesson got me through graduate school and, most recently, became profoundly important for me during the research of my second book. I was studying the Religious Right from the lesbian feminist perspective of the secular left, and aside from discovering what I already knew—that the Religious Right was manipulating religious commitments in the name of capitalist consumerism and conservative political agendas—I discovered something else, something that I wasn't looking for, and something that changed my life—not to mention my research—from the ground up. I discovered that God isn't just a narrative we pick like summer berries or leave for the next person; nor is God a set of social conventions tailored for the weak of mind; nor is God a consumerist social construct who exists in the service of Christian imperialist ideologies and right-wing politics. Rather, I discovered that God through Jesus Christ exists, the triune God of the Bible exists, whether we acknowledge him or not. I discovered that God wasn't very happy with me.

This brought me to the awesome realization that our living God is in all of our life, and that my "success" as a professor was his blessing on me, not my deserved and earned accolade. I discovered, through what the Bible calls the renewing of our minds, that what I had previously claimed as mine wasn't even about me.

This leads me to my point and the title of today's talk: beware of the Solomon problem of academic life. King Solomon, one of the many sons of David, ruled over Israel from 962–922 B.C. Before Solomon stepped into his kingship, he asked God to give him an "understanding heart...to discern between good and evil" (1 Kings 3:9). God gave him a gift of discernment unmatched by any other figure then or now on the condition that Solomon never forgot the first commandment (the commandment to honor God, not the idols that bolster the autonomy of our own egos). As Solomon became rich and successful, he started to believe that knowledge was something that he "owned," something that he harbored inside of himself, rather than what it was: something loaned to him, but something fundamentally located in the radical Otherness of a Holy God. Once he lost his anchor, he lost his wisdom, and it all came tumbling down. The biblical story does not stop here, because the nature of a Holy God is redemptive, not abandoning, but that is a lecture for another day. Suffice it to say for today that Solomon failed by thinking that all truth-claims exist in a contingent relationship to the self. Solomon's legacy offers

> a warning to all academics, believers and atheists alike: we all need to be anchored in something bigger than we are, something bigger than the ideas currently generated within disciplines, and certainly something bigger than the politics of our fields of study.
>
> Real learning, no matter how polished the moves or rehearsed the rhetoric, is empty learning unless we who profess are anchored in something bigger than we are. Choose with discernment, and don't let the proclivities of the here-and-now choose for you.
> —*Syracuse University, August 1999 Graduate Student Orientation Convocation*

I reread this lecture today and it seems so pragmatic and inoffensive. But at the time and place that I delivered it, I had just handed myself the proverbial pink slip. Only R knew how serious this was. After ten years of coming out as a lesbian, you would think I would have gotten used to the feeling of peering over the edge of dignity and choosing instead solidarity with the outcasts. What was different this time was that in giving this lecture, I betrayed my friends. While the lecture itself was not bold, because my friendships were bold and intimate and risky, the lecture had impact. This experience taught me a powerful lesson about evangelism: The integrity of our relationships matters more than the boldness of our words. Because of who I was to the gay community, this lecture had made its mark.

What kind of effect did this lecture have? I might as well have taken out a highway sign that said, "Rosaria is no longer safe—your secrets are out—your cover is blown." While I gave the lecture, I saw my ex-girlfriend and my lesbian- and gay-supporting graduate students go stone cold in disgust and disappointment. Of course, I had talked with them privately before this lecture. But the gay and lesbian community *truly* understands the importance of the public coming-out moment, and therefore, this lecture and its impact resonated powerfully with my people.

After giving my lecture to incoming graduate students, I returned to my office drenched with panic sweat. I felt awkward wearing a dress, and the "girl" shoes I was wearing hurt my feet more than any marathon I had ever run. R left for his office and so I faced mine alone—I also faced a long line of students wanting to talk to me about what I just did.

The only person through my office door that day was an undergraduate named B. B was a skinny boy, high on prescription medication for ADHD, depression, bipolar disorder, and who knows what else. He had been flunking out of school since his first day on campus. B was the president of the Gay, Lesbian, Bisexual and Transgendered undergraduate student collective and I was their faculty advisor. B came to my office to fire me. He was fuming. His eyes were red with tears and his face taut with fury. "How dare you! How could you!" He paced the length of my office; his spike orange hair and red face made him look like a carrot or a cartoon figure. His anger distorted him.

"How do you know that you are no longer a lesbian? How do you know?" he demanded. Of all the questions that someone could have asked me at the time, this was the one that I couldn't answer. This question unsettled me and made me feel sick and dizzy. I had no idea how to answer it. Christ-honoring words and ideas were nowhere to be found. They weren't ready to come out of me. My sense of truth was divided. One truth was simply that the word of God had gotten to be bigger inside of me than I was, bigger by about the size of a hair. The other truth was that, now back at work, I started to feel like a lesbian again. The summer break had helped me to establish new patterns, but these new patterns were flimsy. The patterns of mindfulness of a research professor are well established and they extend beyond reading and writing. Because my scholarship and my personal life shared a symbiotic relationship, the old patterns of mindfulness started to creep back as I sat in my office chair. I had always been both a professor and a lesbian at the same time. My research supported what is called "Identity Politics"—the assumption that the researcher holds integrity when she also holds membership in the area that she studies. Research professors also enjoy being part of a community of scholars. I lost my community when God saved my soul. And now I started to lose my nerve—and my faith.

I tried to stall B and so I asked him a question in return. I said, "B, how do you know you are a gay man?"

Like a birthday balloon deflated by a pinprick, B staggered and collapsed into my office chair. Slumped over and with tears in his eyes, he fell silent for what seemed a long time. Then he said, "Rosaria, I'm a gay man because the GLBT (Gay, Lesbian, Bisexual and Transgendered) community is the only safe home I have, a home made safe by you. How could you not know this? How dare you not know this!"

Although it replicated my own experience, I was taken aback by his response. And I certainly didn't fail to hear that I was fingered in his sin. I don't remember how I responded—right there in my office. I think I covered his hands with my own as he slumped in the chair and cried. I remember that it was dark by the time he left my office and that we agreed to talk again the next day. I accepted my resignation from the student group that he chaired and, later that week, from the other five that I advised. I accepted my resignation from every dissertation committee that I was on and started to dig through my computer and hard files to throw away the book project on the Religious Right. I had to accept it: I was a failure. By God's grace, he would not allow me to work in the way that I had always wanted to labor. I was no stranger to failure, but this was an odd failure. At the infinitesimal core of this failure resided something that I didn't at first recognize. When I examined my feelings against the rugged Cross, I realized that this failure was wrapped in relief. Whatever was God's providence for me, it was his to lay out and mine to obey. No longer did I have to invent myself.

One week later, when the fall 1999 school semester came around, I felt more ready to face the patterns and legacy of my past. My church knew my struggles and surrounded me with prayer and counsel. I had been reading Augustine's *Confessions* and was alert to the reality that God had ministry waiting for me. I prayed that I would be strong for the task at hand. Yes, I was still a laughingstock in the gay community. Yes, I was still a traitor and an example of what not to be. But so too was Paul the Apostle shamed among the Pharisees, and I trusted that God would take my life and make a place for me.

During this time, I lost my primary support person—R left for seminary in Pittsburgh. He felt called to be a pastor, or so he said. We agreed to continue to talk daily and support one another.

During the past six months, I had spent most of my time with him, and while I was sad to see him go, I really needed my time back to focus on my new life as a Christian professor. We had started talking about the emotional attraction we felt for one another. I filed this away, not really knowing what to do with this kind of information. In the gay community, it is normal (and safe) for gay men and lesbian women to bond in this way. But I wasn't in the gay community anymore. Was this still safe? Was this dangerous?

During this time, I also gained a powerful support person and friend—Vivian Rice. Vivian was a professor at the university, a member of my church, and the wife of an elder. Vivian and I committed to praying together at least once a week and talking daily for support and colleagueship. With my church supporting me, I felt ready to face the semester as an "out" follower of Christ.

God did have ministry waiting for me in my classes. The story of my conversion ran like wildfire through the university community. Instead of having fewer students, I had classes that were over-enrolled with students sitting on the floor and in the aisles. Some students came for the carnival aspect, but others came because God had put them where he wanted them. Amazingly, I continued to draw students from the gay and lesbian community, students who wanted to dialogue across differences. I also drew students who were suicidal and chronically sick. As a lesbian, I had always been an outsider. But now I was a different kind of outsider, and in my new status, God brought me a new crop of hurting people.

I couldn't believe how exhausting it was to daily put Christ before me. The old patterns were there waiting for me, and they knew my name. It was so hard to be in charge of a major program at work (as Director of Undergraduate Studies I coordinated the curriculum for over 200 majors) and at the same time be in a posture of submission to my pastor and elders—people I felt really didn't understand the nature or rigor of my work. The only way to effectively ward off the old patterns of selfishness was to put into place intentional Christian ministry. The Thursday night dinners for the gay community were canceled due to lack of interest. Only my drag queen friend J kept coming around and we talked almost exclusively about the gospel. At the same time, some students were openly interested in how God changed me. So I started a Friday night What's-The-Christian-Life-All-About study. I opened my house to anyone who wanted to come and talk about Jesus or ask questions about the Bible. J started coming along with a handful of students and neighbors. One Friday a month we canceled the study and did something good in the neighborhood. It was the motliest Bible study I have ever had the privilege to enjoy.

When R left for seminary, our Christian lives became further divided. While God continued to give me victory over my sin and joy in Christ, R was becoming more and more discouraged. I started to act more like his mother than peer as I gave him counsel and fretted over his problems. When he ran out of money, I sent him mine. When he ran out of phone cards, I sent him mine. He would call me at all times during the night or day. Although this pattern was unhealthy, sick patterns bind people together as firmly as healthy ones do. Before long, we confused fusion by sick patterns with love.

My drag queen friend, J, was the first to talk to me about the "R problem," as she called it. We had gone to a lecture together one night and I was anxious to get home because R had been having a hard day. J kept me talking in the car and told me, firmly, that R was a loser. She really pinned our relationship down when she said, "Rosaria, I know this pattern: he gets deeper and deeper in sin and calls you and you talk him off the ledge. Let him go! Let Jesus deal with him!" I marvel to this day at J's wise and sage advice, advice that I was too proud to receive.

I once asked R if he thought that seminary was harmful to him. I asked him why he felt "called" in the first place. In response, he asked me if Pastor Ken, during the pastoral prayer part of the worship service, still prayed that the Lord would raise up men for the ministry. Pastor Ken, almost every Sunday, prayed Jesus' instruction to his disciples in Matthew 9:38: "The harvest truly is plentiful, but the laborers are few. Therefore, pray the Lord of the harvest to send out laborers into his harvest." He said, "That's why I'm here. I really felt that prayer was for me." I asked him to clarify what he meant: I wondered if R felt that Pastor Ken was directing that prayer to him, or, that the Holy Spirit was speaking to him through Pastor Ken's prayer. I asked because it seemed to me that these were two different "calls"—one directed by man and another by God himself. He thought about it and then told me that he wasn't really sure which "call" it was, after all.

In recent years, I have contemplated this statement, thinking about the difference between the call of God on the one hand (as revealed through the Holy Spirit's work in our conscience) and the call or influence of other people whom we deem powerful or important on the other hand (what Sigmund Freud would call the power of the super-ego). I think about this in the context of church work—about how easy it is for the church to unintentionally manipulate people. According to Freud, the super-ego is the part of the conscious that deeply feels and responds to the expectations that other people and institutions place upon us. The super-ego is our receptor site for people-pleasing. Even as a believer, it is easy to become people-pleasing instead of God-pleasing.

R proposed marriage, and we became engaged in November. We received overwhelming support from the church community. The support we received seemed so extreme and so over-the-top. I've come to note that normally moderate non-pretentious Christians tend towards extreme emotional excess in the areas of weddings and baby showers. This particular weakness had not been mine to witness until I became the object of this attention. I found this kind of attention uncomfortable and annoying. It seemed as though people that I thought were my friends saw me as suddenly more legitimate now that I was going to join the club of the married. I also didn't know to whom or how to articulate my feelings of fear and doubt. Again, I confronted the question: How can a woman like me be a godly woman? I never once thought to ask if R was a godly man. After all, he had shared the gospel with me, bridged the gospel for me, prayed with me and for me. In addition, he was under the care of our session and presbytery and was going to be a pastor. Yes, he was struggling. But if the session knew his struggles and thought he would still make a fine pastor, surely he would make a faithful husband. I had no idea what godly standards of discernment were.

As R and I prepared for marriage, this promise of my first legitimate relationship became very heady for me. I fell more into step with the thinking of my friends at church. He and I talked every day—sometimes multiple times a day. He continued to lose the battle against sin. I struggled over how Jesus could give me liberty and not him, and I concluded that victory was just a matter of time. After all, he had committed (and recommitted) his life to Christ, so what else but victory could be the result? This promise of my first legitimate relationship filled me with pride and awe—the club I had never imagined joining was about to welcome me with open arms. And Jesus, I was sure, would use me in his victory over sin in a special way.

It's a cliché in the gay community but one that I believe is true. It goes like this: Gay men have sex but lesbians have talk. It doesn't mean that lesbians are celibate (although some are), but it does mean that talk is very intimate for women. The talk that R and I shared during this time was too intimate. We started to share the kind of secrets that you can never take back, our mutual histories of sexual sin and family crisis providing more than enough material. I confused all this dredging and sifting with love.

The church's response provided a vast contrast from the university's response. My engagement put my former lesbian community into crisis—again. Former students cried in my office and on my porch. My closest comrades talked to me the way they talked about the deceased at funerals—hushed and careful.

While the women of the church gathered around me to help me plan my wedding, I fretted about what to say to my department chair. What should I do? R had two more years of seminary left, and who knew where he would pastor a church—pastors in our denomination do not get to pick where they live and work. It was unlikely that we would live in Syracuse. Should I quit my job? I didn't want to string the university along while I tried to untangle my personal life. Should I apply for a research leave? I dearly wanted to study Christian education, in part to determine whether I would be a better fit at a Christian college than at a large secular one. I was only eligible for one full-year leave, but he would be in seminary for two more years. Should I try to take a research leave followed by a personal leave? Since my department chair had been such a good friend throughout all my years at Syracuse University, I decided to put the whole matter before him and get his counsel. My department chair was great—encouraging, supportive, helpful. I left his office ready to apply for a two-year research leave. I then went about making plans for renting my house.

The school year went so well. My academic dean approved my two-year leave (first year academic, second year personal). An urban ministry program in Pittsburgh contacted me about teaching in their weekend program. It was all coming together. I felt the power of God in my labor as a professor. I prayed for and with my students. Many students continued to come to my home on Friday nights for a Christian talk-exchange. My classes were all over-enrolled. My classes in Christian Hermeneutics and the Romantic Poets were some of the best classes I had taught in my life. I really felt like I could be a Christian professor. And I really imagined that I could balance being a Christian professor and a pastor's wife. R still wasn't well, but I was sure God would turn it all around before our wedding. I prayed faithfully. The women gave me books about praying for your husband. I was so confident it would all work out.

It's hard to explain what happens when you prepare for your first legitimate relationship, share secrets that you shouldn't, read books about preparing for marriage God's way, lose all your former friends for the promise of one, incur a wealth of disrespect in your work place, prepare a two-year research leave by somehow packaging all of this spiritual trauma as intellectually vital, rent out your house, tie up all the loose ends of directing the Undergraduate Studies program, prepare for a wedding, believe the whole time that what you are doing is God's will for your life, feel love and gratitude for the person who shared over and over again the power of the gospel and who bridged for you life and ministry amidst two warring communities, only to have him come to you one day, and say: "There's something I need to tell you. You can't marry me. I'm not ready. And I'm probably not a Christian."

Here's what I thought: You jerk. You betrayer. You vile, pathetic wimp. I overhaul my whole professional life to correspond with your school schedule and you're not ready? And, you are probably not a Christian? If you are not a Christian, then what are you doing in seminary? If you are not a Christian, then what are you doing behind a pulpit?

How could the person who shared the gospel with me in the most convincing way and whose Christian life most resembled my own "probably not" be a Christian? What did that mean? Was he not "really" a Christian or was he struggling with assurance of salvation? Assurance of salvation means knowing God's call on your life—it means knowing in a conscious way that you are his. We know this through both the Holy Spirit's work in our lives and his call on our hearts. The Spirit's work in our lives is evident through our obedience to God and our love for our fellow man. We find this in the Bible in 1 John 3:10: "Whoever does not practice righteousness is not of God, nor is he who does not love his brother." The Spirit's call on our hearts is revealed in Scripture in Galatians 4:6-7: "And because you are sons, God has sent forth the Spirit of his Son into your hearts, crying out, 'Abba Father!' Therefore, you are no longer a slave (or an orphan) but a son, and if a son, then an heir of God through Christ." To this day, I do not know which he was lacking: assurance or salvation. The Apostle Paul tells us that "Today is the day of salvation" (2 Cor. 6:12). And what about me, what about my faith? How could I "probably" be Christian and R "probably" not be? And what does the word "probably" have to do with it? This was unthinkable.

This conversation happened a few weeks before the end of the semester and our scheduled wedding date.

Like rocks hitting water, the reverberations of shock and sadness came in steady and gentle waves. At the bottom of my crisis was this: Who is this Jesus? Am I following Jesus or R? Whom do I love more? There were other, more practical considerations, to be sure. For example, what was I to do and where was I to live for the next two years? The urban ministry program in Pittsburgh with whom I had just signed a contract worked out of the seminary that he attended. This job didn't pay enough to rent an apartment in Pittsburgh. And my house in Syracuse was rented out to grad students who were only paying enough to cover the mortgage. After addressing the practical considerations, I confronted the personal ones. The rocky underworld of rejection lodged itself in the shaky identity of my godly womanhood. I wondered if somehow R knew something that I did not. Maybe he somehow knew that

I was not healed and that my sexual self would forever be in limbo or worse. How does a single and celibate person even know if she is healed sexually? What is sexual healing? And then if not healed, was I really converted?

I thought about other things, too. Do I break all my promises—urban ministry, research leave, renting my house—and just hole up at home and lick my wounds? These were big decisions fueled by big questions. But the biggest burden on my heart was a problem of worldview: Who is Jesus? Who had betrayed me, R or God? Who is the Jesus who heals some but not others? Who needs a fickle God? Faith is not a feeling. Faith rides the waves of the treachery of life on the Christian worldview that you own. Faith and worldview are intimately intertwined. Our peace, love, courage, longsuffering, and life-works lock-step with our Christian worldview and the faith that undergirds it. Where was mine?

Psalm 15 became my guide. Psalm 15 directed me to keep my promises and showed me how to work in God's strength to do so. In Psalm 15, the psalmist asks the question that burdened my heart—"Lord, who may dwell in your sanctuary? Who may live in your holy hill?" (Ps. 15:1). I needed to know: Was I in God's house? Was I in God's will? Why would God do this to me? The remaining lines of the psalm answered the question I searched for: God's people speak truth (15:2); God's people do not slander neighbors (15:3); God's people fear the Lord (15:4); God's people keep promises "even when it hurts" (15:4, NIV); God's people give money freely (15:5); God's people reject bribes (15:6). The psalm's conclusion offers a promise: "He who does these things will never be shaken" (Ps. 15:5). That's me, I discovered! I'm shaken. My faith is shaken. I prayed that God would help me to live out each line of this psalm, step by step. I finally understood what it meant that Jesus identifies with all of our troubles. I finally believed Hebrews 4:15-16: "For we do not have a High Priest who cannot sympathize with our weaknesses, but was in all points tempted as we are, yet without sin. Let us therefore come boldly to the throne of grace, that we may obtain mercy and find grace to help in time of need." I saw something in myself. By wallowing in pity, I was holding myself back from going boldly to the throne of grace.

The church surrounded me with a gentle presence. No one told me what to do, how to feel, or what to think. The women of my church gave me gentle presence. They enfolded me into their lives and prayers. It took all I had to come to church and not bawl my eyes out the whole time. I felt like I had a year earlier, when the conviction of sin under the preaching of the word was too much and I would leave the service or shut down halfway through. One day, when I started to leave the service early, Elder B followed me out. He said, "Rosaria, it's OK to just pray that God will get you through this moment—this very one, right now." He prayed for me, and God over time gave me the peace to both grieve and survive minute by minute. Another elder-friend invited me to his home for dinner. He and his wife were big supporters of R and they were concerned for him as well as for me. Elder M said to me: "This is the biggest faith test you will ever face. You may face it again in another context, but this is the test that rises as high as we can imagine: Rosaria, Jesus is saying to you, right now, in this moment of shame and defeat, 'Whom do you love? Me or him? Whom do you follow? Me or him?'" I was so thankful for bold elders and faithful praying and grieving friends.

Nobody seemed to really believe that R articulated his lack of faith to me. I suppose the session felt assured of his salvation and believed that he just needed to work on his own assurance. He had a history of exaggerating his emotions and problems, so the session just had him proceed forward, business as usual. The more that I contemplate this today, from a long distance away, married now to a real Christian, I don't think that R was exaggerating. But I don't like the way that my church body handled R's articulation of faithlessness. I don't think we should ever jolly someone into faith, especially someone who has access to a pulpit.

That spring and summer, R was on break from seminary but was expected to continue in his role as pastoral intern for our church. He was assigned to our church plant, in part, I believe, to get him away from me and allow me to worship without (more) distraction. R continued to struggle with people-pleasing. At one point, he sent a letter out to a number of pastors in our denomination, explaining in detail our relationship and our breakup and asking if there was any "sin" in his conduct. As pastors started to debate the issue, privately but within my hearing and the hearing of my friends at church, I truly felt as though an RP alpha-male convention was being played out over my dead body. I felt exposed. I was mortified. I contemplated finding another church.

Although it was not his fault, I felt betrayed by Pastor Ken. I believed he should have warned me about this guy — even protected me from him. Pastor Ken's ministry was unique. In looking back, I see that he wanted to open the doors of the church in a wide way. The doors were wide enough for someone like me to enter and wide enough for someone like R as well. That wide path both served me and hurt me. This crisis made me ask: Had I really been obeying Jesus and following him in faith? The answer was no. No, I had been a double-minded follower of Christ. I followed R who followed Jesus (or, so it appeared). He was my bridge to the gospel, the Bible, the Church, and Jesus himself. These were the incommensurable binary oppositions of my life: 1) Had R not been in that church at that particular time, I would not have kept coming back; and 2) R betrayed me — Big Time.

Sometimes binary oppositions like these are so potentially paralyzing that you just have to put them aside for a while. I tucked this one away for two years. I knew that God calls us to walk in faith, not to be paralyzed by doubt. As Pastor Ken once said to me, "You can't steer a parked car. If you want to turn your life around, you've got to get moving!" It wasn't until recently that God gave me the language and safety to explore what betrayal by a self-proclaimed believer means in God's economy. Pastor Peter Smith said these simple words in a sermon and my ears and eyes and heart and mind opened. Pastor Peter said, "People *will* betray you, but Jesus never will." Much of my past fell in place when he said these simple words. Here is what I gleaned. Betrayal deepens our love for Jesus (who will never betray us). Betrayal deepens our knowledge of Jesus and his sacrifice, obedience, and love. (Jesus was betrayed by his chosen disciples and by all who call upon him as Savior and Lord by our sin.) Finally, betrayal deepens our Christian vision: The Cross is a rugged place, not a place for the squeamish or self-righteous.

I came to learn that summer that God does use us through and in our weaknesses. I came to learn what it means that in Christ "we live and move and have our being" (Acts 17:28). From outside appearances, it looked like the church had betrayed me. And now that, in the court of public opinion, my church had, by all appearances, betrayed me in a public way, I became safe for another group of people. Friends from the lesbian community came back. An ex-girlfriend wrote me a beautiful note (she is a poet). In it, she assured me of her faith in me and told me that I was always welcome back in the lesbian community. She told me not to fear such a hard life lesson and not to think that my old friends want me to suffer. Now that I had a serious faith struggle before me, I became safe for others to share their doubts, fears, and disappointments. My lesbian neighbor had at one point been a woman of faith. I didn't know this. Now she was dying of cancer. She approached me one day and said, "I didn't give a damn about who God was to you in your happiness. But now that you are suffering, I want to know: Who is your God? Where is he in your suffering?"

The phone rang at midnight, or maybe later. As I lay in bed listening to the phone ring, I suddenly remembered that I lived alone in my house and that I would have to answer the phone. I got out of bed, stumbled over Murphy, my dog, and ran down the stairs to the kitchen. I picked up the phone without turning on the light. It was the hospital. One of my graduate students was in the intensive care burn unit. She tried to kill herself by setting herself on fire. I was on her list to call in an emergency (that was news to me). The hospital worker on the phone said, "Oh, by the way, we are putting Paxil in her morphine drip, is that OK with you?" Paxil? Morphine? Why is she asking me this question? I wondered.

I showed up at the hospital and they took me to a room to wash and change. They gave me a plastic bubble suit to put on. They brought me into another room with more plastic wrap and breathing tubes. My student A looked mummified. Nevertheless, she was animated. She thanked me for coming, as if I was an invited guest at a formal party. It was surreal. She was talking nonstop about her fears, her visions, and the fire. She told me that her sister was in trouble—she told me that her sister was involved in a murder and that the murder was part of a satanic ritual. She told me that something bad was after her. She told me that they have male nurses helping her to the bathroom. She asked if she could come home with me. I tried to take it all in. Was this for real? A sister in a satanic cult? Was this suicide attempt a satanic attack? I wondered how a person distinguishes morphine from Satan. I wondered why I was standing there. In that instant I realized: This is God's work for me, right now. Right now, I am to demonstrate the love of Christ to my lesbian student who during this past school year felt deeply betrayed by me. This was God's "right now" calling. I felt shivers run through my body. There is no finer resolution to a faith test than genuine Christian ministry. The still small voice of God was speaking to me, right now, through my student. I was there because God picked me up and put me there. It was time to wipe the sleep out of my eyes and do something.

I put my hand on A's, plastic to plastic, and assured her that I and the church would be there for her. I asked if I could pray for her. She told me I could. I prayed for God's mercy, peace, and saving faith. She fell asleep while I prayed.

I called Ken Smith. I called Vivian and Floy. I called my lesbian colleagues. I called my lesbian students. The lesbian community and the Christian community were going to have to work together for A. A healed—first at my pastor's house and later at my house. I saw the liberty of Christ through her healing. I saw the unity of Christ through the friendships that were born across worldviews in the hospital. I saw the power of Christ when Satan shook A and my household from top to bottom. The elders strongly exhorted me to start to practice what our church called "family devotions"—a nightly time of Bible reading and prayer for the members of the household and its visitors to share together. How in the world does a single ex-lesbian pull off "family devotions" with a satanically suicidal student? Line up all of my dogs and put them in a sit-stay while I opened the Bible? I saw the perseverance of Christ when elders and church members came nightly to my house to help me with family devotions, giving up time that they should have rightly enjoyed with their own families. I saw the compassion of Christ when the children of the church visited A at my home (one asked her if she had ever heard of "fire safety"). A healed. She did not embrace Christ during this time or to my knowledge. But of this I am sure: Christ put his people in her life to do his work of mercy, and we obeyed.

One day, while A was knitting potholders in my living room, R came over. He and A talked privately for a while and after he left, A said, "He's a wacko, Rosaria. All he talked about was his Prozac dosage and his difficulty when the doctors changed it."

Situations like that made me realize a hard lesson: God gives and God takes away and he does it for our good. Indeed, R was both my best friend and no friend at all. I loved him because I confused the sick patterns that we shared with deep personal conviction. But God took him away for my good. God knew better than I did. I—and a whole church of believers—believed that marrying him was God's will for my life. The man to whom I had said "yes" to the most important question an adult can address would have been my ruin had we gotten married. Never again will I think of knowing God's will as anything but the most humbling of acts. And never again will I confuse other people's hopes and dreams for me as proof of God's will.

It was in this spirit of brokenness, upheaval, and exceeding gratitude for God's protection, exactly one year to the day after delivering my Solomon lecture, that I packed my car for Beaver Falls, Pa. As I was loading the car, elder and friend Bob Rice said, "Rosaria, never doubt in the darkness what God has promised in the light." My friend Dr. Ken Smith, at that time chairman of the Board of Trustees of Geneva College, was able to get me a one-year visiting teaching position at Geneva College, our denomination's Christian college. There I would be able to study Christian education while teaching at a real Christian college—and thus keep the promises of my research leave. I was about an hour outside of Pittsburgh, so I would still be able to drive out there on Friday nights and teach in the urban ministry program—and thus keep my promises to my contract. I didn't have to worry about bumping into R at the seminary (where my urban ministry class would meet). God exposed his sins to the session. He would not be returning to seminary. Geneva College graciously allowed me to live rent-free in one of its apartments and the students renting my house covered my mortgage. This allowed me to give back my salary to the urban ministry program, which dearly needed it (Ps. 15:5). And the president of Geneva College even allowed me to bring my dog Murphy. God truly gave me more than I had asked for. His provisions were abundant. My cup overflowed.

Driving away from Syracuse was hard. I wondered if I would ever come back. I loved my white house with green trim. I loved my neighbors. And, at least in the summer, I loved Syracuse. But most of all, I loved my job. With horror, I remembered that I had been willing to give up my job for R. How God had protected me from that man! How could I even consider leaving a tenured professorship! What foolishness! I loved my job and colleagues. Were these gifts or idols? I wondered. With a chill, I knew that if they were idols, then God would, in his love and mercy, destroy them and remove them from me.

My faithful dog, Murphy, licked my face as we got on the highway. I felt exhilarated about what might come next. I was still sad. I was still grieving. I was still praying that R would get it together and come back to real faith and even to me. But no matter what, I was working for God! What a privilege! What an assurance of salvation! God was teaching me how to hold the things of this world lightly. God was teaching me how to use my skills for the Kingdom. God was revealing himself to me through the details of my life and the choices that he put before me. I was driving away from the place, the life, the career, and the people that I knew and loved. But Jesus Christ was more real to me at that moment than any of these material things. Murphy licked my face again and I laughed out loud. This was my conversion in a nutshell: I lost everything but the dog.

The Good Guys
Sanctification and Public Worship

Geneva College, Beaver Falls, Pa., 2000–2001

Somewhere in the process of conversion, I picked up knitting with a vengeance. I have been a knitter all my life, since my Nana taught me when I was six. My post-conversion life found me obsessed with simple, repetitive tasks, and thus knitting became a love, a crutch, a twitchy habit, and the thing that I absolutely could not do without. I loved the feel of wool between my fingers, the material carving a little familiar callus on the outside of my ring finger. I loved the colors. I would pore over knitting books and linger in yarn stores, drinking in the color, breathing in the fiber. I experimented with color and with patterns. I made myself learn how to read a pattern accurately. I found myself reaching for my knitting at all times, but especially when I prayed. I still pray better with needles in my hands. Rows stand for worship, thanksgiving, petition, confession, renewal, people, problems, wisdom, insight, character, memory verses. Some people keep a prayer journal. My prayer journal is knitted into ridges and rows. I can look at sweaters, blankets, mittens, socks, dishcloths and potholders and remember what I prayed about during their birth. I wonder sometimes how much of this is the old habit of praying as a little girl with rosary beads in hand.

Packing to leave Syracuse was filled with terror. I kept my yarn box open, checking to make sure I had brought enough wool to get me through two semesters. I was more careful with my wool than with my clothes. I had planned to be gone for an academic year. I was sure that I brought enough wool for that. Confident that I would return, I left the remainder of my yarn stash, my completed projects, and my personal journals in a box in my neighbor's basement. Syracuse—even with its losses now outnumbering its gains—had become my home. My life as a professor—even with its losses outnumbering its gains—had become my "I am." It was the thing I couldn't imagine living without—my title, my role, my secret place. It was my not-so-secret-stash of self-righteous pride.

I've always been more in tune with the inner landscape of life than with the outer landscape. It takes a lot to get me to notice geographical landmarks or the color shoes that somebody is wearing. I'd make a terrible witness in a crime. While internal landscapes have depth, shape, color, texture and taste, the external world is usually just a shade of gray for me. Even with this deficit in visual acuity, I couldn't help but notice that in driving from central New York to western Pennsylvania, the landscape transformed.

Everything was greener, for one. Trees were lush. The air was moister. My hair started to curl on the turnpike and didn't flatten out until January. As I exited the turnpike and entered Beaver County, something else took me by surprise. The whole county felt "religious." On houses and even businesses, Scripture verses advertised the worldview of the inhabitants. In New York, I was used to seeing pink flamingoes or statues of the Virgin Mary on lawns of neighbors. (I learned that one very important reason to keep my dog on a leash was his propensity to lift his leg on such ornaments, a gesture that did not usually endear me to my neighbors.) Here in Beaver Falls, 1945-style brick bungalows displayed Scripture on placards. (I made a mental note to *always* keep my dog on leash around here.) The most popular verse was John 3:16, "For God so loved the world that he gave his only begotten Son, that whoever believes in him should not perish but have everlasting life." Other houses displayed verses about God's judgment and about the separation of the saved from the lost. It also was an election year. And clearly, I had entered George W. Bush country. Political advocacy plastered next to Bible verses makes me anxious. I'm not a betting woman, but if I was, I'd say that Jesus is not a member of either political party.

It took me a while to figure out how I felt about the Bible verses on the placards. On the one hand, the Bible had become my life, my guide for life, my paradigmatic mirror in which I found meaning and direction. I loved (and love) the Bible, gorging on huge chunks at a time. But these skinny verses, taken out of their rich and complex context, were just sitting out there on placards, naked and rude. I felt an immediate aversion to the aesthetic even as I identified with the message. For example, John 3:16 without John 3:17 seems to balance itself in the wrong place. John 3:17 says, "For God did not send his Son into the world to condemn the world, but that the world through him might be saved." This verse gives me greater clarity into how to read the one that comes before it. It tells me that if Jesus did not come into the world to condemn it, then neither should Christians. The use of the word "might" in the final clause, "that the world through him *might* be saved," tells me that the domain of Christian witness is not salvation (that is God's work) but service—selfless love and sacrifice. John 3:16 standing alone and without the theology of care offered in John 3:17 makes it harder to interpret.

I had learned in a rich and organic way that the Bible webs into all conversations and cultures, like active verbs in sentences or oxygen in the atmosphere. I had learned that Christians need to follow the complex and counterintuitive ways that the Holy Spirit leads. I had learned that being a hero for Jesus was noble work, especially when no one but Jesus himself knew the stakes of the sacrifice at hand. But Bible verses that front salvation over Christian service, instead of being important interfaces between Christian homes and the watching world, seemed like sneaky little raids, quick and insulated targets into culture, with no sense that a worldview of care lay behind them. I had been the beneficiary of real Christian evangelism. Ken Smith spent time with me—and not just spare time. He spent pricey time—real time. He didn't hide behind bumper stickers or slogans. He never let pride masquerade for principle. Perhaps I was being overly reactionary about the new landscape in Beaver Falls. Perhaps I or one of my drag queen friends would be welcome to have a cup of coffee at one of these Bible-loving houses, resting our cups between sips on vinyl tablecloths in country kitchens. Perhaps we would be talked with as people made in God's image. But perhaps not. These placards made me wonder: Would I be welcome because I'm visibly saved? Which is the greater of God's gifts, being made in God's image or being saved, or both? Are we to rank-order these? Are we to treat the visibly saved with greater honor than all of humanity, made as it is in God's image? Do these Bible verses that sit on placards take up the same cultural space as the rainbow flag that once resided on my flagpole? Are these "Welcome" signs or signs that read "Insiders Only"?

Simply put, driving into Beaver Falls gave me the creeps. The placards scared me and the air smelled like Tide laundry detergent and box cake mix behind a backdrop of stale valley-trapped pollution.

I arrived on campus tired and hungry and scared.

At the college's main building, a stranger was waiting for me with a key. He drove me the back way to the place that would become my new home. This second-floor apartment faced an alley that reminded me of the one I used to play Kick the Can in as a child. I keyed in through the basement and entered a large storage and laundry room. I didn't think I would have on-site laundry! This small detail thrilled me. As I walked up the flight of stairs into the living space, the first thing that I saw was a beautiful rocking chair. I love rocking chairs and was sad to leave mine in Syracuse. I scanned the place. A tidy kitchen, a soft couch, a comfortable bed, a desk, and even a TV (a much larger and nicer TV than I had!). The carpet was clean and the kitchen had a fresh coat of white paint. I put Murphy's dog bed between the bedroom and living room. I sighed. I had to face it. This place was simply perfect. God has led me to my perfect home. I sang Psalm 23B to myself while I unpacked the car and took Murphy for a walk in our new neighborhood:

The Lord's my Shepherd, I'll not want;
He makes me down to lie
In pastures green, he leadeth me,
the quiet waters by;

My soul he doth restore again,
And me to walk doth make
Within the paths of righteousness
Ev'n for his own name's sake.

Yea, though I walk in death's dark vale,
Yet will I fear no ill;
For Thou art with me and Thy rod
And staff me comfort still.

A table Thou hast furnished me
In presence of my foes;
My head Thou dost with oil anoint,
And my cup overflows.

Goodness and mercy all my life
Shall surely follow me;
And in God's house for evermore
My dwelling place shall be.

I fell into a deep and peaceful sleep. I felt like a little child, fully dependent on someone wise and knowing. I had grown used to thinking that I was taking care of myself. Leaving my faculty post, even temporarily, was my way of saying, "Lord, I'm yours; give me what you will have me to hold." There, as the fog of sleep receded, I experienced something that I simply could not conjure up in my consciousness: I experienced peaceful trust.

The enormity of the risk I had just undertaken didn't hit me until I woke up for the first time in Beaver Falls, hearing trains, church chimes, and cardinals. Where was that trust that I had felt in my sleep? Why didn't obedience produce trust? I contemplated this: Could it be that obedience is somehow easier than trust? This is the point that begins Jerry Bridges's book *Trusting God Even When Life Hurts*: The boundaries for obedience are clear, but trust must somehow manifest itself in the boundary-less world of "anything can happen." The fact that God is sovereign over the good and the evil does not necessarily make the evil any less frightening. I recited Psalm 23 and got myself out of bed.

It was Psalm 15 that got me to Beaver Falls and Psalm 23 that kept me there.

For my birthday that year, Floy had given me a little book by F. B. Meyer called *The Shepherd's Psalm* (1889). In it, I found what we in English studies call a controlling metaphor (a powerful albeit understated idea that holds all the other parts of a paradigm together). This, I believe, is the controlling metaphor of the Christian life, and one that I first found in Meyer's book and first seized in that little cozy apartment during my first day in Beaver Falls. Meyer says, "Unbelief puts circumstances between itself and Christ, so as not to see Him....Faith puts Christ between itself and circumstances, so that it cannot see them" (p. 17).

When I woke up to my new life in Beaver Falls, it was the Lord's Day. My first order of business was to choose a church. I had moved to the Mecca of the Reformed Presbyterian denomination. In Beaver Falls alone, there were five RP churches—two within walking distance, two within running distance, and one approachable by car. I never did find this last RP church, although I have it on good report that it exists. My plan was to visit each of the RP churches and then to transfer my membership to the one where I believed I would grow in the knowledge and grace of Jesus Christ and in my service to the church and to the world.

That morning I worshiped at the RP church right across the main street of Geneva College. The face of this church was different from Syracuse. People were younger and more casually dressed. Most of the people in attendance were Geneva College faculty, retired faculty, staff, students, or alumni. I had never even heard of this college until I united with the RPCNA. Now it seemed that everyone in my vicinity attended it at some point or another. I had never lived in any community that was quite this ingrown.

The new academic year was about to begin, and all the before-church-service-buzz was Geneva College Shop Talk. People re-hashed the humanities curriculum, building plan, lack of raises, concerns with the administration's handling of this and of that. The sharp edge of the conversation was different than I had expected. Because we are such a small denomination, I expected that we all got along! Silly me! The talk here was local, personal, and sometimes conspiratorial: The conservatives have taken over the seminary! The Truly Reformed were alienating Christians from other denominations! Some presbytery thought that it owned the college and was trying to impose adherence to a literal 24-hour-six-day creation standard that violated the academic freedom of both Reformed and non-Reformed faculty!

I had been on faculty, as a graduate student, non-tenured professor, and tenured professor for over a decade and I had never heard faculty talk like this. I could not have been more confused if these folks started talking Telugu. I felt a slow panic bleed through me. I knew how to be a professor. I knew (barely) how to be a Christian. But if understanding the *lingua franca* buzzing around me was necessary to function here as a Christian professor, then I was dead in the water.

Some people probably learn how to swim by falling off a boat and almost drowning. But that doesn't necessarily mean that they would make great swim coaches. I felt like someone whose Christian life was born in this kind of death-or-life tug-of-war. I was just coming to my Christian senses. I hadn't written my testimony in a way appropriate to share with strangers. I felt like a non-native speaker trying to communicate the most important and complex truth in a tongue I barely handled. My embryonic biblical literacy crumbled under the weight of the expectations around me.

My most sincere prayer that morning at this church was that no one would ask me a question whose depth or merit extended beyond "Would you like a cup of coffee?"

This early introduction at the pre-service talk time typified my time at Beaver Falls. This would be a year of tearing down and melding together, of tossing out and grafting to the Cross. Grief makes us fickle, as we try on our self-diagnosis from all points of view. What ails me? My broken engagement? My feminism? My church community's naïve relief in resolving my past homosexuality in my future heterosexual marriage? My past sexual sin? My present sin? My driven covetousness of a life built on something other than bad choices? Here I was in a public setting and I didn't have a game face to put on. These people with their complete marriages, their kind children, their well-spent lives cast a reflection on the legacy of my choice-making. I wondered how different my life would have been had I gone to Geneva College. Would I have met the Lord as a college student? When I used my old worldview, my life felt like a cruel joke. But I knew even then that God's providence was neither arbitrary nor fickle. God allowed me to rise as high as I could and fall swiftly and publicly. Had my sin not preceded me in a public way and had my repentance not been my lifeboat, had I found myself neatly protected within the confines and choice-making of Christian family and community, I today would probably have been the greatest of all Pharisees. Some people are smart enough to learn lessons the easy way. Not me. I always need to fall on my face.

Folks at this church were friendly. I was immediately welcomed to join the women's Bible study and given many slips of paper with phone numbers to call if I needed anything. (My phone would not be hooked up for weeks to come, as I moved to Beaver Falls during the Verizon strike, but I valued the sentiment nonetheless.) From the church bulletin I could tell that this church was as committed to outreach as to caring for its own members. And although they were at the time in search of a new pastor, they didn't appear to be divided, angry, or confused. The retiring pastor was preaching that day. Dr. Jonathan Watt has a PhD in linguistics and was on faculty at both Geneva College and our seminary. He was leaving the pastorate to commit himself to full-time teaching. His sermon was shorter than Ken Smith's and much more polished.

I had gotten used to the fact that in every Ken Smith sermon, my still-kicking feminist sensibilities would be offended—deeply. Ken used the male pronoun exclusively and once used "totalitarian" throughout a whole sermon when he really meant to say "totalizing." I was seething. And, oddly enough, I kept coming back for more. Was I a masochist? I wondered. Or was I learning to forbear? I came to believe that my job was not to critique and "receive" a sermon, but to dig into it, to seize its power, to participate with its message, and to steal its fruit. I learned by sitting under Ken Smith's preaching that the easily offended are missing the point. At the Syracuse church, my colleague and friend Dr. Ken Smith taught an adult Sunday school class. In Dr. Ken's class, I was learning how Christians make priorities. I was learning to examine my gender politics against the teachings of Scripture. I was learning that it was safe to do this, and that even Bible-believing Christians upheld a range of possible biblical applications to the question of gender and women's roles. But here at this church I found a more sophisticated message and a more sophisticated audience. I didn't leave the sermon feeling raw. I left the sermon thinking about literature and the rich array of languages that webbed through a biblical worldview. It got me thinking about biblical literacy in new and deeper ways. The service was short and to the point. The pastor was very warm and kind. Part of me loved this place and part of me didn't trust myself here.

In Beaver Falls, the Reformed Presbyterian churches offer not just morning services, but evening worship services as well. This was a new tradition for me (and one I had a hard time incorporating). My usual pattern in Syracuse was to don my pajamas after supper and curl up in bed with a good book. The churches in Beaver Falls all had different identities. The church that I had visited that morning felt like the company church—it was for professors and students—the young, cool, hip and happening people. For evening service on that first Lord's Day in Beaver Falls, I walked the two blocks from my apartment to the Geneva Reformed Presbyterian Church. The pastor at the Geneva Reformed Presbyterian Church was Bruce Backensto. I had heard that Bruce was working on a PhD in theology on the doctrine of sanctification, and that he and his wife, Kim, both had prior divorces.

I entered the church building ten minutes early—my usual for a first time visit anywhere. I stayed to the back and listened to people talk. The buzz here was about a woman named Mary Lou who was fighting liver cancer. A match had just been found and the operation was to take place soon. Years of prayer carved this long and painful journey. God has heard the prayers of his people.

Once spotted, I was greeted by people who made me feel like old friends: There by the church kitchen were Willard McMillan and Renwick Wright, and their dear wives, Shirley and Maureen. They welcomed me as if they were waiting for me to come. I had met both couples in Syracuse where their grown daughter and son and grandchildren lived and worshiped. There was nothing hurried here. No pretenses. Willard said, "You've been through so much. Are you well? Is God sustaining you?" Renwick said, "Here is our Daniel, David and Paul all in one! Has our Lord given you victory today? If not this whole day, how about this very minute?" I felt immediately safe to explore my fickle and unstable heart. I hoped that here at the Geneva church, it was safe to grieve. I couldn't impress anyone here if I tried, so I settled into the hard work of turning the pages of my heart, holding each one open and naked for spiritual scrutiny.

The service was about to begin and we took our seats in folding chairs in the damp and moldy church basement. The congregation consisted mostly of people in their 70s and 80s. The only visible exception to this was the pastor's large and young family. There were also a few college students and a handful of 20- and 30-somethings. The psalm singing was the most dreadful that I had ever heard, with hearing aids bumping and crashing the already-unstable pitch at each stanza. There was one old gentleman who insisted on holding on to the note from one stanza until the next was well under way. The singing made me dizzy in a seasick kind of way. Bruce walked to the podium with a lurch and a limp uncharacteristic for a man who appeared to be in his fifties. His presence in the pulpit was intense and urgent. He seemingly had no notes. He was preaching from Galatians 5:16-25:

> So I say, live by the Spirit, and you will not gratify the desires of the sinful nature. For the sinful nature desires what is contrary to the Spirit, and the Spirit what is contrary to the sinful nature. They are in conflict with each other, so that you do not do what you want. But if you are led by the Spirit, you are not under law.

> The acts of the sinful nature are obvious: sexual immorality, impurity and debauchery; idolatry and witchcraft; hatred, discord, jealousy, fits of rage, selfish ambition, dissensions, factions and envy; drunkenness, orgies, and the like. I warn you, as I did before, that those who live like this will not inherit the kingdom of God.

> But the fruit of the Spirit is love, joy, peace, patience, kindness, goodness, faithfulness, gentleness, and self-control. Against such things there is no law. Those who belong to Christ Jesus have crucified the sinful nature with its passions and desires. Since we live by the Spirit, let us keep in step with the Spirit. Let us not become conceited, provoking and envying each other. (NIV)

The focus of this sermon series, Bruce explained, was to explore in detail each of the deeds of the flesh, and to examine ourselves in the light of this Scripture. Today we would explore, in explicit detail, the first deed of the flesh mentioned: sexual immorality.

As I sat in that folding chair and listened to Bruce preach, I knew that I had never heard anything like this. It corresponded to Scripture, and to what I had been reading in the Bible. But I had never heard anyone talk like this from the pulpit. In Syracuse, we only talked like this in private, and then, only with some people (never Pastor Ken). Pastor Bruce was eagle-eye direct, painfully honest, and unapologetically bold. There was no question in my mind, as the tears started to run down my face: I had just barely started on the journey of my repentance. And here I had thought that I had repented in full and that my pain was the result of R's sin. Ha! This sermon hit me hard across the face: I was suffering from my own sin, from the pride that was still rising high in my heart, and from my false sense of entitlement and deserved goods. Here I had spent the summer feeling and acting like some innocent victim of a random crime. How false! I was guilty.

R's sin was on his head, but I had much of my own sin to both claim and shed at the throne of Grace. One of the complexities of repenting from sexual sin is that its consequence is double-directional, casting a shadow on both our past and our future. It affects the way we remember (and rationalize) and the way we live. I felt completely transfixed by Bruce's message. I was scribbling notes as fast and as furiously as I could. I felt like someone parched gulping water in panic and frenzy. As I was trying to keep up with this unfamiliar style of preaching, Willard McMillan passed a note down to me from his folding chair row. He winked at me when a stranger placed it in my hand, so I would know that it came from a friendly place. The note said: "Hang in there and keep breathing!" I looked up and over to him, and he beamed that melting smile that made his eyes dance like falling stars. In the hue cast by Willard's dancing eyes, I knew it. I had now found my church home. After the benediction, which I sorely needed, I unfolded myself from my chair and I walked to the door. I was too wiped out to talk to people or to thank the pastor. The usual niceties of church were completely lost to me that night.

I was drenched with sweat and had used up all my Kleenex. I walked the two blocks to my apartment slowly and gingerly, as if injured. Never in my life had I had a spiritual experience like this. I felt like I had just come as close as I ever had to understanding the living Jesus. I wanted my friends in Syracuse to hear what I just heard. I felt both vindicated and convicted. I felt peace. Walking home in the dark, it became perfectly clear to me why God brought me to Beaver Falls, the real reason, the best reason. The Lord brought me to Beaver Falls to sit under Bruce Backensto's preaching and to live out what I was learning. I had much more sin, layers of sin, from which to repent. And through Bruce's preaching, I would learn how to grieve through repentance without feigning false innocence. I learned that night the simple truth of sanctification on this side of heaven: it is as the writer of Hebrews tells us, both "already" and "not yet." Even when faced with the blinding sting of someone else's sin, it really is not someone else's sin that can hurt us. It is our own festering sin that takes the guise of innocence that will be the undoing of us all.

I spent my first week in Beaver Falls trying to catch my breath. I was incommunicado. No phone. No e-mail. I wrote a letter to Ann O'Neill, to let her know that I was in town and that my phone wasn't working. Ann lived in Pittsburgh and her husband, Jerry, was (and is) the president of our denomination's seminary. Although I had only met them a few times, they both maintained the rigorous faith that I wanted and that I admired. They reached deep into the world and touched people that most conservative Christians don't even know exist. I could tell that by the way that they welcomed me. They gave me good counsel when R broke off the engagement. They were no strangers to suffering. They were the kind of people that could handle someone else's grief without taking things personally. Getting to better know Jerry and Ann was one of the things that I was most looking forward to in my new life in Pennsylvania.

My first week at Geneva College was startling to me. Faculty culture is always a deeply peculiar thing. I had grown comfortable with the faculty culture at Syracuse, where it was OK to not like each other. Here was another story! Many of the faculty were themselves Geneva College alumni. I was (and am) suspicious of this. It seemed to me that former students (even if now faculty members) would not exercise the proper liberty when debating their former and beloved professors. Instead of bringing a fresh look with new angles to the curriculum, the student culture and the faculty climate, I feared that these former-students-now-professors would be swayed by nostalgia, sentimentality, and respect for authority. Instead of growing into their own professorial identity, I suspected that many young faculty were trapped in their mentor's identity. Or maybe I was just jealous of the fact that these people still had a career while I had just flushed mine down the toilet.

My schedule looked like this. I team-taught one Critical Theory class with another Geneva College faculty member. I taught a senior seminar on Charlotte and Emily Brontë in the context of Christian hermeneutics. During the week I also conducted independent study classes and led one campus Bible study. Students at Geneva presented a wider range of college preparation compared with my Syracuse undergraduates. The students welcomed me with an intensity that surprised me. They shared with me the many conflicts that are universally faced at Christian colleges: denominational fighting and cultivation of sin, both big and small. One big issue was how the Catholics and Protestants would get along. On the first night of Bible study in my small apartment, one student turned to another and said, "You're Catholic? What are you doing here?" The Catholic student responded: "Twenty percent of the student body is Catholic! The question is: 'You're RP? What are you doing here?'"

Well, this was surely going to be an interesting place! Monday through Thursday was filled with students filing into my office, trailing me to the cafeteria, coming to my apartment for Bible study, and helping me find my balance as a Christian and as a professor.

One of the Herculean feats of my schedule was my weekly commute into Pittsburgh to teach at the Center for Urban Biblical ministry. The challenge was getting there. Pittsburgh is littered with rivers, tunnels, and one-way streets. Driving to Pittsburgh from Beaver Falls required transporting oneself through the land-equivalent of the Bermuda Triangle.

This treacherous journey was well worth its dangers. The single most important and life-changing experience of my academic life waited for me at the other end. At the Center for Urban Biblical Ministry (CUBM), I worked for a no-nonsense black woman named Karla Threadgill Byrd, and I taught courses in the Bible as Literature and Research Methods. My students were all much smarter than I was. Each person there had a story—or ten. Each was a jewel in Christ's crown. My students were black and, more often than not, over 40. They were putting their lives together after much hardship. In spite of poverty, racism, and lack of education, my students found the time to be foster parents, parents, students, and some pastors. (I'm sure that my husband and I are licensed foster parents today and parents of four children-of-color because of the fine and godly example that these saints gave to me.) When I drove from Beaver Falls to Pittsburgh on Friday afternoons, and when I stepped into my classroom, no matter how tired or discouraged I was, I knew that I was entering holy ground. If I ever go back to teaching, I would consider it an honor to work again at CUBM and for Karla Byrd. CUBM was a desperate place. We weren't trying to impress anyone—least of all, each other. We tried, with humility, to hear God's call on our lives and muster the courage and integrity to fulfill it.

My work at CUBM ended late on Friday nights. I was grateful when Jerry and Ann O'Neill offered extended hospitality—to me and my dog! After teaching, I could go to the home of Jerry and Ann, for dinner, for prayer, and for the best sleep I would have all week. Each Friday night, Jerry and Ann spent time with me—again, pricey time, not spare time. They allowed me to integrate into their family, to spend time with the children who were still young enough to live at home, to watch a Christian family function. I stayed at their home every Friday night for that whole academic year. I shared with them everything. No matter how late into the night we talked, we always ended the evening with prayer. Their home was my safe haven, and their friendship helped hold me together week after week. I would return home Saturday afternoon refreshed and ready for the Lord's Day. On some weekends, I would join them for worship at the Providence RP Church. I was taking it all in, everything from content of sermons, family dynamics, personal styles in ministry and life, roles for women, loss, healing. Like Ken and Floy, Jerry and Ann allowed me to experience with them real Christian living.

One month into my new life, a faculty colleague approached me asking if I would like to be part of a lecture series on the integration of faith and life. I was intrigued. I hadn't found my public voice yet in this strange Christian climate, and this seemed like a good place to start. I accepted the invitation and decided to give my "Solomon" paper, revising the introduction to explain its context and its original audience. Since my paper was already written, I agreed to give it the following week.

I was shocked that many faculty colleagues came out for these talks. At Syracuse, I would have been speaking to an audience of about three. The unspoken rule among the overachieving faculty at Syracuse was clear: if the activity didn't beef up the Curriculum Vitae, then don't do it! I was doubly shocked to see Pastor Bruce there. The difference between giving the same talk at Syracuse and then again here at Geneva College was startling to me. At Syracuse, I was speaking as a traitor and an outcast. Now, I was speaking as an insider to other insiders. People responded with support and encouragement. As I was reading my paper, I felt sort of like I was floating on the ceiling watching myself deliver the paper. I recalled my deep traitorship to the gay community. I started to feel that weak-kneed nausea that had accompanied its first delivery at Syracuse. My talk felt flat and unimportant. I felt like I was making a fool of myself.

Two very important things happened after this talk, both related to counseling. As the audience was filing out, Pastor Bruce approached me and asked if I was OK (I wasn't) and if I needed weekly counseling (I did). Bruce is direct, if not blunt, and I have always appreciated this about him. We set up a weekly counseling time. For that whole year, Bruce and Kim spent hours with me, listening to my journey and helping me to see God's providence in its twists and turns. They shared their own journeys, and I saw bits and pieces of their lives and of the Rugged Cross that Bruce shared in his sermons. He wasn't just writing a dissertation on sanctification; he and his family were living it. Had Bruce and Kim charged me by the hour for their time and counsel, I still would be paying back the debt I owe to them.

Second, Dr. Dean Smith, chair of the Bible Department (and former pastor of the College Hill RP Church, a church with a long history and equally long solid reputation), asked me if he could help me in any way. He had noticed that I wasn't OK and invited me to his office to talk. I spent time—a lot of time—in Dean's office that academic year. I told him that I felt like an impostor and that I didn't know how to be a Christian professor. I asked him if he would mentor me and if I could sit in on a class of his, to see him teach and to learn how to integrate my faith and my life. Dean's warmth and his vulnerability put me at ease. He and his wife, Nancy, brought me into their home during times that would likely be hard on me. I spent the best Christmas Eve of my life in their home (even though, for several reasons, I didn't then and don't now celebrate Christmas). Dean welcomed me to audit a class he was teaching in Christian counseling, and it was in Dean's class that I first learned how to study the Puritans. It was also in Dean's class that I saw a real Christian professor at work. I was amazed at the levels of integration (of discipline, knowledge, Christ, hardship, betrayal, perseverance, compassion, and faith) that I could discern in Dean's lectures and his manner of dealing with students. I didn't then and I don't now have this gift. Dean's gift is tangible and ethereal. He moves fluently between preaching and lecturing. He redeems every student question. He humbles himself, but only gains respect in doing this. I was mesmerized by his biblical fluency, his emotional intelligence, and his humility. I tried to take notes about Dean's giftedness as a professor, to see if I could apprehend even a kernel of it. I'm still working on this today. I had spent my best years steeping in the wrong worldview. God saved me, but hadn't lobotomized me. My deep patterns of thinking and interpretation were also suspect to sin. That was painfully evident to me now.

After two weeks in Beaver Falls, God assembled for me a powerful team of Christian counselors and role models. Pastor Bruce taught me to apply the means of grace that God provides to repent and to grow in sanctification. Jerry and Ann taught me to pray even when I didn't feel like it. Karla taught me to sacrifice and take risks. And Dean modeled for me how one grafts "Christian" and "professor" into one.

After I thanked God for my teachers and role models, and after I started praying risky and bold prayers, he sent me ministry—students, in packs, hungry and searching and real.

A month or so after my Solomon talk, the college chaplain approached me with a proposition. He was putting together the schedule for a chapel-sponsored grab bag called Convocation (sometimes lecture, sometimes praise and worship songs, etc.). Students were required to attend a certain number of chapel services and convocation lectures, so I was guaranteed a good turnout. (If this was said to make me feel better, it didn't.) He wanted to know if I was ready to share my testimony with the college community. "No thanks," I said. "Really," he said, "Think about it." I didn't have to think about it. I was having a hard enough time living my testimony. And I had seen too many Oprah Winfrey shows, where one off-her-rocker contestant after another claims salvation-through-something. And I had read too many cheesy Christian testimonies, all written in the past tense, all very simple, happy, and filled with more clichés than sugar in Grandma's cookies (or, in my case, garlic in Nana's meatballs). I decided to excuse myself from the myriad of rhetorical snares implicit with the sharing of one's testimony. My conversion still felt like a train wreck, and I am averse to clichés on any level. I decided to vow silence.

All of the testimonies that I had heard up to this point were egocentric and filled with pride. Aren't I the smarty-pants for choosing Christ! I made a decision for Christ, aren't I great? I committed my life to Christ, aren't I better than those heathens who haven't? This whole line of thinking is both pervasive among evangelical Christians and absurd. My whole body recoiled against this line of thinking. I'm proof of the pudding. I didn't choose Christ. Nobody chooses Christ. Christ chooses you or you're dead. After Christ chooses you, you respond because you must. Period. It's not a pretty story.

"Pray about it," the chaplain said.

I did pray about it, so that I could with good conscience say no. I was reluctant to make myself a poster child for gay conversion. I felt and feel no solidarity with people who think their salvation makes them more worthy than others. I didn't want to call attention to myself. I didn't want every wacko on campus to confess his or her feelings of same-sex love or homophobia or refer for counseling their gay aunts or neighbors. I thought about the bumper sticker once popular in the gay community as a spoof against evangelical Christians: "I killed a gay whale for Christ!" Or the other bumper sticker, "Lord, please protect me from Your people!" I still felt ambivalence about my disloyalty to my gay friends. And I knew that I could not write a neat, happy, schmaltzy, G-rated, egocentric testimony if my life depended on it.

But, I wondered, could I write an honest testimony? Could I, in the Apostle Paul's words and tradition, write and deliver a testimony that reveals repentance as fruit of the Christian life? In English studies we have a mantra: A culture is comprised of its stories. "We are the stories we tell," I've said to my students year after year. I was critical of the stories I heard from my churchy friends and my evangelical culture. But could I be more than just critical of the stories that encompassed me? Could I start a new conversation? What would happen if I just told the truth? Was anybody else out there ambivalent about conversion? Did anyone else see it as bittersweet? Did anyone else get lost in fear when counting the costs of discipleship? Did anyone else feel like giving up? Did anyone else tire of taking up the Cross daily? Did anyone else grieve for death to one life that anticipates the experience of being "born again"? Did anyone else want to take just one day off from the command that we die to ourselves?

I told the chaplain the next day that I was ready to give my testimony to the campus. "But," I warned him, "My testimony is R-rated."

I gave myself a month to write and revise the ten-page paper that became my testimony. I put up pictures of my old friends in my apartment and I pictured myself delivering this paper in front of them. I panic-wrote in the early dark mornings and revised late into the dark night. I held every thought captive to the truth. I prayed that, in telling the truth, God would be honored.

I don't have a copy of the testimony that I first wrote and delivered at Geneva College in the fall semester of 2000. When I walked into the auditorium, it was packed and noisy with the energy of student life. I remember being relieved that Pastor Bruce and most of the elders of my church were there to support me. Someone introduced me, and I stepped up to the microphone. I began the talk by asking if anyone knew the difference between the concepts "private" and "confidential." I told them that what I was about to tell them was private. Private things can be discussed in special circumstances, but not in common ones. There-fore, if students wanted to talk with me about what I was about to tell them, they needed to schedule special time. I was not go-ing to address what I was about to say in my classroom or at the lunch table. This is hard for me, I told them, and they are to respect my boundaries about this. They listened well. I remem-ber feeling the visceral respect that a speaker feels when a room suddenly goes tear-dropping quiet.

I shared my life. I told them the real truth as best as I could. I remember feeling great dread as I read from my prepared manuscript.

The talk generated a lot of questions. Some questions revealed what these students had not learned about God's grace. One stu-dent asked: "How do you know you are healed if you are not having sex with a man?" In return, I asked him, "Why is my health as a Christian determined by having sex at all?" I went on to explain what has always seemed obvious to me, but often comes as a great shock to Christians. I explained that too often good Christians see sexual sin as merely sexual excess. To a good Christian, sex is God's recreation for you as long as you play in God's playground (marriage). No way, José. Not on God's terms.

What good Christians don't realize is that sexual sin is not recreational sex gone overboard. Sexual sin is predatory. It won't be "healed" by redeeming the context or the genders. Sexual sin must simply be killed. What is left of your sexuality after this annihilation is up to God. But healing, to the sexual sinner, is death: nothing more and nothing less. I told my audience that I think too many young Christian fornicators plan that marriage will redeem their sin. Too many young Christian masturbators plan that marriage will redeem their patterns. Too many young Christian internet pornographers think that having legitimate sex will take away the desire to have illicit sex. They're wrong. And the marriages that result from this line of thinking are dangerous places. I know, I told my audience, why over fifty percent of Christian marriages end in divorce: because Christians act as though marriage redeems sin. Marriage does not redeem sin. Only Jesus himself can do that. The audience seemed a little shocked to hear this.

The questions shifted from sexual sin to expressed anger at church culture: specifically, how do we talk like this in church when church is, according to one student, "filled with hypocrites." Although only one student articulated this sentiment, the auditorium sighed with solidarity. I pointed that out to them and asked for a show of hands to better see how many shareholders this idea had. The majority of the audience raised a hand. I then put my manuscript aside and issued a challenge to these students. "Maybe churches are filled with hypocrites because you are not there. Or maybe churches are filled with hypocrites because you are there in pride and in self-promotion. Here's my challenge to you: For those with church ties, start going to church in honest vulnerability. For those of you who are not going to church at all, come to church with me. Make a six-month commitment. Pray with me for God's saving and guiding grace, and then we can talk about whether or not church is filled with hypocrites."

I should tell you that I rarely speak off of my manuscript and that when I do, I always get myself in trouble. This was the dumbest charge I have ever issued in a public forum.

After this talk, a group of students organized to take me up on my offer. These were students who were doubting, or unbelieving, or deep in sin, or seeking real ministry hoping to support fellow students who were ready to ask honest questions of the church and of the Lord. I started bringing with me to the Geneva RP Church a troupe of students. The church was grieving the imminent death of one of its younger members. Mary Lou, in her early sixties, for whom a liver was matched and ready for transplant, could not accept the match because cancer had already hijacked her life. The church had prayed for years for Mary Lou to have a donor. God's will in this situation seemed like a trick or a bad joke. Pastor Bruce, preaching through Romans, was highlighting the mystery of God's will and the overriding power of God's character. Pastor Bruce was preaching through Romans in the morning and Galatians 5 in the evening. My students and I watched Pastor Bruce preach and watched a congregation grieve.

After church, we came back to my small apartment and addressed basic and fundamental questions: Why shouldn't I have sex before I'm married? Who is God to say that my body is not my own? How does my internet sex really hurt anybody else? What do I do with my past? My family? My friends? My depression? My addiction? My anxiety? After a time of discussion and prayer, we took a walk with my dog and reassembled for evening worship.

What we did, these students and I, for a whole academic year, is very simple. It is called "Sabbath keeping," and my denomination values it highly. We simply took a day off from real life so that we could explore and expand our spiritual lives.

During this time, colleagues and friends continued to pose to me questions that I had avoided answering. These questions were about my church's worship standards (sometimes also called the "distinctives" of the Reformed Presbyterian Church of North America) and about why I believed such worship standards were indeed biblical. My colleagues wondered why such bizarre worship standards were not off-putting, especially to unbelieving students, and why a postmodern gal like me could abide by them. One colleague put it succinctly: The RP Church's worship standards lack New Testament grace.

I had to face these questions head-on. I didn't want to. I liked my church. I liked my pastor. I liked my history with Ken and Floy Smith. I felt and feel connected to my denomination because of emotional and experiential attachments.

These questions from my colleagues made me squirm. I felt like a lightning rod for confusion and suspicion about the RP Church. I was asked at a faculty meeting if I was a plant for the RP Church. (At the time, my friend Dr. Ken Smith was Chairman of the Board of Trustees, and, I assume, my new colleagues at Geneva felt that I was reporting directly to Ken.) I was told by a department chair that my denomination was "exploiting me for my testimony" and once they found out who I really was (who *am* I? I wondered, and how did this guy think he had me figured out?), they would "run me up the flagpole and light a match." I was told by a retired biblical feminist that I should leave this patriarchal denomination for its unbiblical gender politics and find my spiritual niche in the Episcopalian church, perhaps as a priest.

I was asked—time and again—to explain why I was a member of the Reformed Presbyterian denomination. It was a good question, but a hard one. The question hurt because it touched a raw nerve. I knew that I was Christ's, but I really didn't know why I was a member of this denomination. At the time, all I could say was, "These are the people that God sent to come get me, and I'm loyal as a bird dog!" Well, loyalty is fine and good (especially for a bird dog), but real Christian intellectuals expect (and rightly so) more than that. Why am I a member of this denomination? I wondered. And why are those things that set us apart in worship so alienating to others? Why do people think that I am not "using my gifts" in the worship of God if my church doesn't let women preach or sing solos? Do I have to perform in a church service in order to participate in it? Do performers grow in grace more strongly than participators? It seemed to me that, in worship, God wanted me to sit down, shut up, and listen—so that I could go and use my gifts out there in the world. It did not occur to me that God wanted me to show off or bring attention to myself. But even this was just an impression, a sensibility. I had nothing solid to say to anyone who inquired: Why are you RP?

I started to ask other people who worshiped in the RP Church these questions. Many people seemed untroubled by these questions. Many of my RP colleagues took a "live and let live" attitude about the worship practices that divided us. Indeed, some of my RP colleagues were even apologetic about our worship practices. Many of my colleagues were "blue bloods"—that is, members of families that have a long lineage in our denomination. It seemed to me that their "membership" was never under the kind of scrutiny that mine was. There was only one person who took my questions as seriously as I did: Kent Butterfield, then a seminary student. He recommended two important books to examine: Michael Bushell's *Songs of Zion: A Contemporary Case for Exclusive Psalmody* and Brian M. Schwertley's *Sola Scriptura and the Regulative Principle of Worship*. Through the study of these books, I became convinced that the worship of the Lord was the most important thing that we can do. Notice: I did not say that it is the *only* thing that we do. But worship is the launching pad for life. And, through it, God equips us to do Kingdom work in the world. Therefore, worship has to be right in God's eyes and right in our hearts and minds. Through the study of these books I fell in love and gratitude with our denomination's worship standards, seeing them as foundational—not to our salvation, but to our sanctification and our service.

These questions led me back to my first intellectual love—hermeneutics—and to a book by a Christian scholar named Kevin Vanhoozer, entitled *Is There a Meaning in this Text?: The Bible, the Reader, and the Morality of Literary Knowledge.* It seemed to me that I had to grasp these questions about worship practices from the point of view of hermeneutics. "Hermeneutics" is an old Greek word that refers to how we interpret life, text, and events. That is, hermeneutics is the study of how we make meaning out of text. Another word that often interchanges with hermeneutics is worldview. Hermeneutics focuses on the details; worldview takes the point of view of the frame. These two terms need to be understood in relationship. A stained-glass window relies on the right relationship between the details that make up each frame and the big picture that emerges when you lift your eyes off the minute detail. It is exceedingly dangerous to build a Christian life on just one or the other. You must hold both in tension and balance. Taken together, hermeneutics and worldview make up a critical perspective. Is there such a thing as a Christian critical perspective on worship? I wondered.

As a feminist scholar, this concept—worldview—was the most important concept in my intellectual arsenal. Worldview is central to feminist studies and to any field of study that analyzes oppressed or marginalized peoples. It helps us to understand how interpretations come from the frames of intelligibility that we use to look at the events that matter. Critical perspective asserts that we make meaning out of our lives not by personal experience but by the frames through which we filter that experience. On my Women's Studies 101 syllabus, I wrote this about critical perspective:

> NB *(nota bene,* or, "note well"): Students are expected to write all papers and examination essay questions from a feminist worldview or critical perspective. In Spanish class you speak and think in Spanish. In Women's Studies you speak and think in feminist paradigms. Examination essay ques-

tions written from critical perspectives outside of feminism will receive an automatic grade of F. Papers written from critical perspectives outside of feminism will be allowed one revision. Any student who is unable to write and think from a feminist critical perspective or worldview with a clear conscience should drop the class now.

How did I get away with this? The secular academic world is bold in its protection of worldview. And, I and all of my feminist colleagues put this statement on our syllabi. We worked as a bloc. We comprised an interpretive community. An interpretive community consciously and intentionally protects its way of thinking. This is how important worldview is to education—of all stripes and colors. And this is how important interpretive community is to worldview. We do not make meaning in isolation.

But is worldview really that important? Doesn't life teach us lessons on its own terms? My students and I often discussed this question. My students and I often discussed it like this:

Let's take, for example, a teenager who keeps getting into trouble with the police and with the rules at school. Parents want to teach this child that cause has an effect. Parents may think that the best way to teach this kid a lesson is to let the school of hard knocks, i.e., life, be the teacher. But the problem with this is it assumes that these "hard knocks" stand on their own. Everything filters through a worldview. Let's say this kid's worldview is "I can only trust my friends. All people in authority (parents, pastors, teachers, police, etc.) are out to get me." With this worldview, the harder the knocks, the more firmly this worldview gets hammered home. And of course this kid's choice of peer group—his interpretive community—helps him see all "hard knocks" as proof that people in authority are out to get him. Maybe this kid will turn out like the Prodigal Son. But how did the Prodigal Son come to his senses? The Prodigal Son didn't repent of his sin because he got tired of living like and with the pigs. He repented because God gave him eyes to see. Until this happens, no personal experience can topple his critical perspective. That's the thing about the frame we use to look at the world. It is actually stronger than life experience because it is mindful, positioned, owned, established, and deeply held. Personal experience can seem fickle. Worldview (the end result of the critical perspective we choose) is always intimate and claimed.

What are the elements of a Christian critical experience? The Bible, the individual denomination or church's practices and traditions, and the personal experience of the believer. But because different denominations rank these elements differently, there really is no such thing as "a" Christian worldview. The question, then, for me, was: How do we in the Reformed Presbyterian Church assemble our worldview? What goes first, my personal experience as a believer or the church's doctrines? The Bible or the church's traditions and practices?

At the time that I was struggling with these questions, I was reading and teaching from *Is There a Meaning in this Text?* Specifically in the context of worship, Vanhoozer's book helped me formulate my problem with the questions that my colleagues were asking me. The right questions are important. As any college sophomore can tell you, you can't produce the right answer on a final examination if the professor asks the wrong question. My colleagues were asking me about worship and how it related to my personal experience. Asking a former heathen like me if I missed the hymns in formal worship is like asking a cannibal if he misses tofu. I had no personal template for worship. It was all foreign, all uncomfortable, all well outside of my experience. Vanhoozer's book helped me dispense with the wrong questions so that I could focus on the right ones.

The right question is this: Do we have a biblical mandate for our worship practice? If God tells us how to live, does that include providing specific warrants for how to worship? Living out our Christian lives takes creative thinking, as we try to split the hairs of prepositions, as it were, and live in but not of the world. Fluency is always creative, slangy, and contemporary. But the question is this: Is my biblical fluency stronger or weaker in the context of a worship service that includes room for creative additions to the worship of God? Are we better off? Is God pleased with our creativity in the context of worship? How much creativity does God want? Yes, interpretation matters, yes, interpretation is messy, but is there a biblical warrant for worshiping God in specific ways? If so, how tightly does God draw in the boundaries? These questions could only be answered by understanding the hermeneutics of some basic teachings in the Bible: the authority of Scripture—*sola scriptura*—and its logical consequence for worship—the Regulative Principle of Worship. These questions forced me to focus on other devices central to textual studies: on canonicity (to understand *sola scriptura*) and genre (to understand exclusive psalmody).

My use of literary devices here may seem very technical. But I remind you that I am an English professor by training. My training prepares me to think highly about how a text is assembled and to respect its authority. But it shouldn't only be "my training" that matters here. As Christians, we follow Jesus. Jesus is, as John's Gospel explains, "the Word [who] became flesh, and dwelt among us" (John 1:14). Many Christians, to their great deficit, have never thought about the importance of Jesus as the word, or about the Bible as a literary text. Many Christians, to their great deficit, have never thought about genre and canonicity. I find these literary devices invaluable in understanding the Person and Work of Jesus Christ and in approaching Jesus in formal worship.

I turned then to the literary device called "canonicity" and to Brian Schwertley's book, *Sola Scriptura and the Regulative Principle of Worship*. Schwertley is a hard read. He is harsh in his caricatures of others. Nevertheless, his book taught me a lot. I don't mind being offended if I grow in grace through the sock in the chops. Schwertley's point is this: The consequence of *sola scriptura* (the belief that the Bible is authoritative, complete, perfect, and sufficient) is a principle that regulates worship. This principle has the following components: proof texts from the Bible and a hermeneutic or a way of handling these proof texts. The proof texts that Schwertley asserts are these:

> Deut. 4:2—Do not add to what I command you and do not subtract from it, but keep the commands of the Lord your God that I give you.

> Prov. 30:6—Do not add to his words or he will rebuke you and prove you a liar.

Deut. 12:32—See that you do all I command you; do not add to it or take away from it. (NIV)

What principles about worship are derived from these verses? If we believe that God in his Bible teaches us how to live, then it is principally true that God also teaches us in his Bible how to worship him. Importantly, what regulates worship is a principle—an overarching idea—not a specific verse in the Bible. The regulative principle requires that you handle the whole Bible, sifting its details for its overarching principles. If you read your Bible the way unbelievers read their horoscopes, you can't mine the book for principles.

While the Bible is inerrant, the doctrine of *sola scriptura* does not deny "the diverse means of divine revelation before the close of the canon" (Schwertley, p. 11); and does not deny that "there were many revelations and historical events that did not make it into the canon" (p. 11). In other words, the Bible has been "canonized." That means that certain texts by divine appointment have been admitted into a place of authority, which, by implication, means that other texts, while written and available, have not, by divine appointment, been given this authority. The Bible comes to us as a text edited by men through God's divine power. This point requires a big intellectual leap: the Bible is the only book edited by God himself. But, and this is important, while the Bible is true, it does not contain all lessons we need to know in the world—God expects us to learn from life. The question then is this: Should worship practices be derived from our experiences in life? Our tastes? Our cultural values? If we believe in *sola scriptura*, we have to say no. Worship is separate from life and worship standards must come from the Bible—that is, they must come from divine revelation and not from natural revelation.

This may be a hard pill to swallow. Worship is regulated by God's authority, and, for that reason, we are to do what God commands and not add to it in the formal worship of God. This doctrine does not deny the value of learning from life. Each person must seek to learn God's lesson from God's providential struggles, sufferings, and joys. But—and this is a "big but"—this doctrine does "fence" the worship of God—it places a special boundary around it, for its sacred protection and for our own. The more God-centered our worship practice, the more mercy-centered our life. Worship is our rehearsal for how to live today and how to glorify God in heaven. It is not merely a Sunday morning exercise meant to make us feel good. Upholding the Regulative Principle puts real pressure on real issues: In an RP Church, you will get no show, no comedian pastors, no rock bands, no skits, no videos, no interpretive dancing. Either Jesus comes to worship with us and the Holy Spirit fuels and fills us and God is honored, or we have, simply, painfully, nothing at all.

Finally, I turned to the literary device of genre to better understand the "distinctive" of the RP Church that is often most critiqued: our adherence to *a cappella* psalm singing to the exclusion of all other music of praise. The book that helped me to understand our position on psalm singing is Michael Bushell's *Songs of Zion*. The literary principle that undergirds an understanding of the Regulative Principle of Worship is canon: The Bible is canonized. The literary principle that undergirds an understanding of exclusive psalmody is genre: The books of the Bible are organized as all books are under genre. A genre is a "style or category (of text) characterized by a particular form and purpose" (*OED*). The word "genre" and the word "gender" share an etymological history. Just as genre has a specific purpose, so too does gender. If we care about genre—and we should—then we have to grapple with the question: if God gave us a book of praise songs, who are we to add to them? Bushell points to exclusive psalmody as the logical consequence of *sola scriptura*. Why? First, because of the importance of the genre of the Book of Psalms within the scope of the canonized Bible. Second, because, as the high priestly prayer of Jesus in the seventeenth chapter of the Gospel of John declares, it is the word of God alone that directs our lives and purifies our desires and our prayers. Jesus says in his prayer to our Heavenly Father:

> Sanctify them by Your Truth. Your Word is Truth. As You sent Me into the world, I also have sent them into the world. And for their sakes I sanctify Myself, that they also may be sanctified by the truth (*or, the word*). (John 17:17-19)

The Psalms are the word of God. While hymns and praise and worship music take up themes of Christian life, we are told very clearly here that we are sanctified by the word and by the word alone. Themes may educate and inform, but only the word sanctifies and directs and discerns and convicts:

> For the word of God is living and powerful, and sharper than any two-edged sword, piercing even to the division of the soul and the spirit, and of joints and marrow, and is a discerner of the thoughts and intents of the heart. (Heb. 4:12)

Because Jesus Christ is alive and sits at the right hand of God the Father, interceding on behalf of his people, and even singing with us as we worship God, we know that we believe in a God who is personal, alive, compassionate, and involved in our day-to-day and moment-by-moment concerns. What does Jesus likely sing with his people in worship? What did Jesus sing two thousand years ago? The Psalms.

Because the Psalms are dialogic (they pose questions and offer answers), psalm singing involves learning the meaning, purpose, and grace that undergirds each individual's life calling, and living under the faithful presence of God's guiding Hand. This manifestation of aesthetics, the study of what makes something beautiful, bittersweet, compelling, and enduring, imbues each note of each psalm. The Christian life becomes a symphony of aesthetics, as each note resounds and resonates to God's glory and, by the Hand of his composition, fits together, even during those times of darkness and struggle, those times when the symphony rings cacophony. In singing the Psalms, in worship and in life, we always know where God is in our suffering. In singing the Psalms, we always have a song in our heart that provides us with direction, redirection, rebuke (when needed), and encouragement. After years of singing the Psalms, and because the word does not return void, we listen, we respond, and, as part of God's training of our hearts, we grow in grace and sanctification.

The Psalms are the words of Christ. Christ is the word (*logos*) made flesh. Because Jesus calls himself the word made flesh (and not the "theme" made flesh or the "paraphrase" made flesh), we take him at his word. We do not rewrite or revise God's word. Rather, we live it. We live it when it fills us with joy. We live it when we are frightened. We live it in his grace. We live the word and it endures through each personal trial and each disappointment. We live the word and it endures through the faithful presence of God's Holy Spirit working through us. His faithful presence becomes our faithful presence. It is known through the senses, like the oil on Mary's hair, oil that she rubbed into our Savior's cracked and pained feet, and oil that she wiped off with the most intimate resource she had: her own hair. Wherever Mary went, the faithful presence of our Savior and the memorial of her love for him followed her. We step into that faithful presence and its palpable aesthetic as we sing psalms.

I had come to the close of my first leg in the study of this material. This is rich terrain, and I am still studying this today. And the more I study, the more I believe that God commands us to sing psalms in worship to the exclusion of man-made hymns.

And what about that Kent Butterfield who directed me to such important books and who took my spiritual questions and needs so seriously? Well, to quote my favorite 19th-century heroine, Jane Eyre, I have only this to say about Kent Butterfield:

"Reader, I married him."

4

The Home Front
Marriage, Ministry, and Adoption

Beaver Falls, Pa., 2002, and Purcellville, Va., 2002–2009

I could fill a whole book about Kent Butterfield—if he'd let me! I could tell you how his soft brown eyes put me immediately at ease. I could tell you how his outstretched hand placed on my lower back dissipates the tension from the day. I could tell you how his practical jokes still stump me. I could tell you about the time that I celebrated the departure of two weeks of back-to-back needy houseguests. One guest from the group would root me out of the bathroom in constant need of detailed and specialized kitchen equipment: "Rosaria, where is your Pampered Chef garlic press (spring-form pan, electric rice maker, water-filtering system)?" I commemorated her absence by taking a long shower with the bathroom door unlocked. Suddenly, the door opened. I felt a rush of cold air and someone said, in a voice I couldn't place, "Mrs. Butterfield? Where is the Williams Sonoma cappuccino maker?" I screamed! Kent confessed his joke. It is a good thing that his outstretched hand cures the twitch in my back, because his practical jokes assemble the plucky comic relief of our life in ministry and our marriage.

Kent is my husband, my best friend, my prayer partner for life, and my one true love. But, alas, dear reader, I cannot write a whole book on Kent Butterfield. He is too humble and modest to allow it. Or perhaps he is too fearful about the details that I might share! Either way, you will have to make do with the book that continues here.

How did a woman like me ever get married? I do not know many feminists who hold the institution of marriage as radically negative or dangerous as I had in my past. While I was researching the Religious Right in the early 1990s, I subscribed to some Christian women's journals. My favorite was entitled *Adam's Rib* and was published by the Promise Keepers. My lesbian friends and I would pore over this magazine and howl in laughter at its absurdity. I could not imagine people with two or three synapses still firing in their neuro-pathways that could live this way. The pictures in the magazine seemed right out of the 19th century. And the issues these women addressed? My three favorites were these: Should women wear pants (no metaphor intended), should women be college-educated, and should the 19th amendment be repealed? That marriage was slavery, as first feminist Mary Wollstonecraft declared in the 18th century, was never more obvious to me than in the pages of *Adam's Rib*. (Of course, the title for me and my friends was worthy of a few good cackles too.)

Before I became one of Christ's own, this was how I viewed the institution of marriage: as dangerous and as something to be avoided. When the subject of "gay marriage" would come up among my friends, I would respond by asking, "Why add good people to a sick institution?"

Kent and I were married on May 19, 2001, in the church where Kent had graduated from seminary the night before. Our wedding was simple—cold cuts from Sam's Club and sweet ice tea by the gallons. We even rearranged and reused the flowers that were "gently used" by the previous night's ceremony!

Our wedding was officiated by two pastors: Pastor Bruce Backensto and Pastor Doug Comin. Doug was Kent's pastor and Bruce was mine. Before I met Doug, a colleague warned me about him like this: "Rosaria, had he met you before you were converted, he would have stoned you to death before asking the first question." After I had met Doug, read a selection of his sermons and books-in-progress (he is one of the most prolific writers I know), sat under his preaching for a season, and had the privilege to get to know his family (including spending our daughter Mary's first homecoming at his home for Thanksgiving), this caricature of Doug became even more baffling. Doug is his own man and a gifted scholar as well. I had friends like Doug in graduate school: they could make high theory out of pepperoni pizza and juggle fourteen Modern Language Association interviews without popping a pimple. Doug is super smart and his ability to put his finger on the pulse of sin and just hold it there can knock your socks off. His capacity to weave a text together, layering Scripture upon life premise or pain, so that the end result is neither intellectual nor experiential but something both deeper and wiser, is unsettling. Doug has slow-motion impact. Doug's integrity silently commands a response-in-kind.

One component of Christian weddings in the Reformed Presbyterian Church is something called the "biblical charge." In it, the pastor charges (i.e., commands or exhorts) the groom and bride to remember God's authority in creating the institution of marriage. I quote here in full, with the author's permission, the biblical charge written and delivered to us by Pastor Doug Comin at our wedding:

> Dearly beloved, we are *not* gathered here today in order to observe a social convention devised by human wisdom for the mutual comfort and happiness of men and women.
>
> Nor do we assemble here to participate in a mere tradition which has come down to us from ages past and which we have deemed to be worth preserving among ourselves.
>
> We are gathered in this place in order to acknowledge, celebrate, and solemnize the divine institution of marriage, which is ordained by the Creator and Savior of the world, sealed and governed by His authority, and entered into by His people with humble obedience and heartfelt rejoicing for the wondrous provision of the Lord for their mutual happiness and completion.
>
> It is the popular misconception of marriage as a mere social convention or quaint tradition invented by the brain of man which has led to the denigrating of this holy relation,

the multiplication of unspeakable immorality, the common unrest between husbands and wives, and the gradual disintegration of society and civilization.

For if marriage exists merely by human authority then men and women may do with it or conduct themselves in it as they please. They may redefine it, or they may abandon it altogether. But if marriage is a divine institution, then it is governed by a higher authority. It becomes, then, a matter of obedience, and the conduct of husbands and wives within marriage is a conduct for which they must give their account to God.

The original institution of marriage is therefore basic to our understanding of marriage, our estimation of marriage, and our right behavior in marriage.

The fact that marriage is a divine institution is emphasized in the very beginning of God's written revelation. The creation of the human race was not complete until the institution of marriage was sealed by God Himself.

And the Lord God said, "It is not good that man should be alone; I will make him a helper comparable to him." Out of the ground the Lord God formed every beast of the field and every bird of the air, and brought them to Adam to see what he would call them. And whatever Adam called each living creature, that was its name. So Adam gave names to all cattle, to the birds of the air, and to every beast of the field. But for Adam there was not found a helper comparable to him. And the Lord God caused a deep sleep to fall on Adam, and he slept; and he took one of his ribs, and closed up the flesh in its place. Then the rib which the Lord God had taken from man he made into a woman, and he brought her to the man. And Adam said, "This is now bone of my bones, And flesh of my flesh; she shall be called Woman because she was taken out of Man." Therefore a man shall leave his father and mother and be joined to his wife and they shall become one flesh. (Gen. 2:18-24)

There are many important truths contained in these verses, and time does not permit us to address them all on this occasion. Several foundational facts, however, may be noted:

1. It was "not good" for the man to be alone. He was incomplete, and what was necessary to make him complete was his wife. Men and women are not independent individuals who happen to share the same dwelling. They are mutually dependent upon one another and each is incomplete without the other.

The Apostle Paul applies this truth of the mutual dependence of men and women when he writes:

But I want you to know that the head of every man is Christ, the head of woman is man, and the head of Christ is God....For man is not from woman but woman from man. Nor was man created for the woman but woman for the man....Nevertheless, neither is man independent of woman, nor woman independent of man, in the Lord. For as woman came from man, even so man also comes through woman; but all things are from God. (1 Cor. 11:3-12)

2. God made Adam experience the fact that he was incomplete. It was necessary for the man to be made aware of his incompleteness before God brought his wife to him. Had this not been so, he would tend to regard her as a nice, but really unnecessary addition to himself. He would view her as something that he could take or leave. But God prepared him to receive her—and treat her—as one who was necessary for his own completion.

3. Adam was utterly passive in the institution of marriage. God made him fall into a deep sleep, and while the man slept, God created the woman who would make him complete. Since marriage is by God's design, and not by man's, it is plain that marriage must conform to God's will.

4. The woman was created by God with special "hands on" care, which signified her special nature as a creature made in

the image of God. Someone has written, "The woman has had a long history of being trampled on. This has especially been the case in heathen civilizations. She has differed little from the cattle that a man owned. Even in the church the notion has prevailed with some that the wife is a lowly creature, fit to bear whatever abuse the man might pour on her. Men have disdained their wives as if this were true piety, because the man is head of his wife. Every such notion and practice is cut off by the account of the woman's creation in a position of high honor."

5. The woman was created, not from the dust of the earth, but out of the very substance of the man. Adam recognized her as "bone of his bones, and flesh of his flesh." Jesus emphasized this truth and its implications:

> And he answered and said to them, "Have you not read that he who made them at the beginning 'made them male and female,' and said, 'For this reason a man shall leave his father and mother and be joined to his wife, and the two shall become one flesh'? So then, they are no longer two but one flesh. Therefore, what God has joined together, let not man separate." (Matt. 19:4-5)

The mysterious and intimate union which God designed between a husband and wife is the reason that the dissolution of marriage, whether by divorce or by death, is such a painful and devastating experience. The separation of a husband and wife is like the severing of a part of the body. This truth also has important implications for how husbands and wives are to treat one another, as we will see.

The original account of creation, then, lays the groundwork for marriage as a divine institution for the mutual good of men and women in order that they may be complete. But even more important than the happiness of men and women found in this union is the fact that marriage was instituted in order to fully manifest the image of God. Thus we read in Genesis 1:27, "So God created man in his own image; in the image of God he created him; male and female he created them."

The union of men and women in marriage is therefore put forth in the Scripture as a mirror, or image, of the relationship between God and his people. In the Old Testament God speaks of Israel as a bride which he betrothed to himself, and the New Testament portrays the Church as the Bride of Christ. This truth forms the basis of Paul's commands to Christian husbands and wives concerning their mutual duties toward one another:

Wives, submit to your own husbands, as to the Lord. For the husband is head of the wife, as also Christ is head of the church; and he is the Savior of the body. Therefore, just as the church is subject to Christ, so let the wives be to their own husbands in everything. (Eph. 5:22-24)

Paul's instruction begins with the duty of the wife toward her husband, which is to "submit to him, as unto the Lord." Elsewhere, wives are told to be obedient to their husbands. The reason for this submission and obedience, according to the Scriptures, is that the wife is to be a living illustration of the Church in its submission to Christ. When a wife refuses to live in submission to her husband, this picture of the Church's relationship to Christ is distorted before the world.

Submission refers to the inner attitude of the heart. It is therefore invisible and secret. Obedience is the outward expression of submission seen in the behavior of the wife. A wife may outwardly obey her husband and yet inwardly despise him. She is, therefore, not in submission to him in spite of her outward behavior. If this is the case, then the picture presented is no different from those who go through the motions of religious activities and yet have no regard toward Christ in their hearts.

True religion, which is pleasing to God, is obedience which flows from the humble submission of the heart. Anything less than this in religion is hypocrisy. Likewise, that which pleases the Lord, and illustrates the beautiful relationship between Christ and his Church, is a humble submission of the heart of the wife to her husband, which results in outward obedience to his will.

This does not mean that she must do everything that he says, for Paul makes it clear that her submission is to be "in the Lord." She is not bound to obey her husband, therefore, if he requires her to sin against God. Yet in all things that do not violate the word of God, the wife is not to overrule, oppose, or contradict her husband. By God's design, she stands in relation to her husband as the Church stands in relation to Christ. The Church is not the ruling head over Christ, but the obeying body, and the wife is to imitate this relationship toward her husband.

"But what if my husband is unreasonable?" This cannot be said of Christ, but it may certainly be said in regard to many husbands.

"Am I bound to submit and obey even if my husband is clueless?"

> Wives, likewise, be submissive to your own husbands, that even if some do not obey the Word, they, without a word, may be won by the conduct of their wives, when they observe your chaste conduct accompanied by fear. (1 Pet. 3:1-2)

God's word is clear. Even if your husband is an unbeliever, your purpose is not to make him submit to you, but rather to win him to submission to the Lord through the example of your own humble conduct so that he is won "without a word."

The "fear" of which Peter speaks is not fear of the husband, but fear of the Lord. This is why Solomon's description of the virtuous woman says, "Charm is deceitful and beauty is vain; but a woman who fears the Lord shall be praised."

To a God-fearing wife, it is important that God's word not be blasphemed, especially on account of her. Paul wrote to

Titus that the younger women in the Church were to be taught "to be discreet, chaste, homemakers, good, obedient to their husbands, that the word of God may not be blasphemed."

He understood that the conduct of a wife in marriage presents a picture of the Church's relationship to Christ. For a wife to be indiscreet, unfaithful, independent, unhelpful, and disobedient to her husband would therefore reflect upon the glory of Christ.

Let all of your conduct as a wife, therefore, be governed by this understanding—you represent before God, before your husband, and before the world the humble character of the Church in relation to Jesus Christ.

Now to the husband, Paul writes:
> Husbands, love your wives, just as Christ also loved the church and gave Himself for her, that He might sanctify and cleanse her with the washing of water by the Word, that He might present her to Himself a glorious church, not having spot or wrinkle or any such thing, but that she should be holy and without blemish. So husbands ought to love their own wives as their own bodies; he who loves his wife loves himself. For no one ever hated his own flesh, but nourishes and cherishes it, just as the Lord does the church. (Eph. 5:25-29)

Again, the instruction is based upon the reflection in marriage of the glorious relationship between Christ and his Church. Here, however, we find that the husband stands not in the place of the Church, but in the place of Christ as he relates to his wife.

Immediately, the sinful pride of man begins to assert itself! This is wonderful! That means that I am the head! I am the boss! I give the orders and she must do what I say!" But wait! The word does not say, "Husbands, *rule* your wives as Christ rules the Church." It says, "Husbands, *love* your wives as Christ loved the Church, and gave Himself for her."

The first thing that we must understand is that "love" is not put forth here as a feeling or emotion. The world defines love in this way, but the Bible speaks of love not in terms of feeling but of action. Love "does this" and love "does not do that" for the promotion of the good of its object.

When God says, "Husbands, love your wives," he is not commanding you to feel a certain way toward them — he is commanding you to act in a certain way toward them, regardless of how you feel!

And how did Christ show his love for the Church by his actions?

> For even the Son of Man did not come to be served, but to serve, and to give His life a ransom for many. (Mark 10:45)

> Greater love has no one than this, than to lay down one's life for his friends. (John 15:13)

He was willing to sacrifice everything for the welfare of his Bride, not looking to his own welfare, comfort, happiness, or fulfillment, but surrendering all of this in order to bless her and make her complete.

Such a husband is not difficult to submit to! But a husband who takes the role of a tyrant toward his wife will only provoke her inclination to resist him. What is worse, when a Christian husband lords it over his wife in a harsh and unloving manner, he declares to the world that Christ rules over his church in the same way.

There is no doubt that the Scripture teaches the husband's headship over the wife in marriage, for Paul clearly declares "the head of every man is Christ, the head of woman is man, and the head of Christ is God." And again he says, "For the husband is head of the wife, as also Christ is head of the church."

Yet the role of the Christian husband, according to God's design for marriage, is not to press his headship or to assert his rule, but rather to demonstrate it according to the pattern of Christ. He is to love his wife in the same way that Christ loved the Church—that is, by self-sacrifice. Test your love toward your wife by the Scripture's own definition of love in 1 Corinthians 13:

Love suffers long and is kind.
When you are tempted to be impatient and harsh with your wife, remember the infinite patience that Christ has shown toward you, and continues to show on a daily basis.

Love does not envy; love does not parade itself, is not puffed up.
When you are tempted to be jealous for preeminence over your wife, remember Christ who did not think it beneath himself to wash the feet of his disciples.

Love does not behave rudely, does not seek its own.
When you are tempted to insist upon your own way, and belittle your wife, remember the condescension of Christ, who left the glorious habitation of heaven, clothed himself with flesh, and endured the shame and suffering of the cross all for the sake of your own helpless, hopeless soul.

Love is not provoked.
When you are tempted to raise your voice in frustration against your wife, remember Christ, who "when he was reviled, did not revile in return."

Love thinks no evil; does not rejoice in iniquity, but rejoices in the truth.
When you are tempted to judge her motives, or to exalt in being proven right when she is in the wrong, remember Christ who had every right to think evil of you and to rejoice

in your destruction, but instead took your shame upon himself and covered you with his righteousness.

When you are tempted to belittle your wife, or to sit quietly while others tear her down, remember Christ, who comes to the defense of his sheep and stands between them and the accuser.

Love bears all things, believes all things, hopes all things, endures all things.

When you are tempted to throw in the towel, and surrender hope that your marriage can continue—when conflicts mount and it seems that it would be easier to walk away than to persevere, remember Christ who bears your sin daily in order to cause your hope to persevere until the end, and who promises "I will never leave you nor forsake you." The love of Christ for his people is not based upon any worthiness within them, nor should your love toward your wife be conditioned upon her actions and your judgment as to whether or not she has earned your love.

Love never fails.

Therefore, what God has joined together, let no man separate. In all of these things, and in many more ways, the self-sacrificial, loving headship of the Christian husband mirrors the love of Christ for his Church. This is your calling as you enter into this sacred union. But there is more.

Paul speaks of the purpose for which headship has been committed to the husband in marriage. It is for the edification of his wife in all purity and holiness. Your role, then, as a Christian husband, is to nurture your wife in the faith, and to provide for her spiritual as well as her physical welfare. Christ ever lives to make intercession for the saints. You must, therefore, pray constantly for and with your wife. Christ nourishes his Church with the milk and meat of His word. You must therefore minister the word to your wife, and teach her to know the deep things of God.

Finally, Paul summarizes the whole matter with these words:

For we are members of his body, of his flesh and of his bones. "For this reason a man shall leave his father and mother and be joined to his wife, and the two shall become one flesh." This is a great mystery, but I speak concerning Christ and the church. Nevertheless let each one of you in particular so love his own wife as himself, and let the wife see that she respects her husband. (Eph. 5:30-33)

"In the world," it has been said, "marriage is a battlefield on which a vicious, relentless struggle rages between the tyrant-husband and the rebel-wife. Now the one, now the other, is temporarily victorious. At present in our society, the rebellious woman has the upper hand. If the world lasts, the male will again assert himself, overthrow the woman's dominance, and rule her more tyrannically than before." (David Engelsma, *Marriage, The Mystery of Christ and the Church*, p. 66)[3]

Over and against this stands God's glorious design of Christian marriage, in which husband and wife are joined together as one flesh—not competing individuals vying for supremacy—each fulfilling an essential role and together manifesting the wondrous beauty of God's love, care, and provision for his precious Bride to the glory of Jesus Christ.

May our Lord so bless this union, that it is a living and true portrait of the mystery of Christ and his Church.
—*Married by God's Design*, Pastor Doug Comin

I quote this text in full because it shows that in Christ anyone can have a good marriage. Jesus is an equal opportunity Prophet, Priest and King: He equips, strengthens, forgives, comforts, and brings into fruition the reality of sanctification. Jesus can equip anyone—no matter how lost or broken—for godly living. I'm living proof of that.

I also quote this text in full because, like our vows for membership in the Reformed Presbyterian Church of North America, it still startles me. I still hear this text with the ears of both an insider and an outcast.

As a newly married Christian woman, I had to confront this dual point of view, this insider/outsider identity. I also had to confront something that may seem so obvious it is not worthy to mention: I had to confront my age. I was 39 years old when I married Kent. I was too old to have children (without fertility treatments). This was startling to me. I had spent my childbearing years fighting windmills and now I was, yet again, waking up to my life. There is a biblical principle that lies behind my confusion: People whose lives are riddled with unrestrained sin act like rebellious children. Sin, when unrestrained, infantilizes a person. Here I had thought that I was so mature, so capable, so "important" in the world, and the truth remains that I didn't even know how to act my age! After conversion, I was surprised to discover how old I really was.

When you come to Christian marriage from a feminist perspective, the most difficult idea to embrace is that of a husband's headship and a wife's submission. When I'm looking at this paradigm from a secular perspective, it smacks of the abuses of patriarchy. But when I'm seeing it through Christ-centered eyes—as Doug Comin's biblical marriage charge exhorts—Kent's headship and my submission have been a source of comfort and solidarity. When Christ is at the center of our marriage, Kent's headship and my submission have allowed us to be a functional team. When Christ is at the center of our marriage, we don't struggle with what Ken and Floy Smith have identified as a major antagonist of Christian life in our century: a "right-of-choice" mentality. When Christ is at the center, each major decision does not throw us into crisis. Each joy and each danger does not make the walls of our relationship crumble.

I don't mean to imply that I have never felt oppressed or undervalued by my role or that Kent has never felt overburdened by his. We are human. And our feelings, like the rest of our being, are fallen too. We each have struggled with our roles, more in the first year of our marriage than today. But when we are in sync, in Christ's center, together we are like a hammock, bearing the weight of our labors and ministry in the most efficient way. When we got married, Ken and Floy gave us a copy of one of the books that they have written. It is called *Learning To Be a Family*. The twelve chapters of this Christian workbook outline the picture of the happy family found in Psalm 128. Ken and Floy's book helps me to articulate—even when I can't manifest or apply it—the process and the balance of what it means to be a happy family. A happy family is not one where each member gets to do his or her own thing. A happy family fears God and strives for obedience. Psalm 1, in its entirety, outlines the happiness, prosperity, and enduring good reputation that a person receives in obedience:

> How blessed is the man who does not walk in the counsel
> of the wicked,
> Nor stand in the path of sinners,
> Nor sit in the seat of scoffers!
> But his delight is in the law of the Lord,
> And in his law he meditates day and night.
> He will be like a tree firmly planted by streams of water,
> Which yields its fruit in its season
> And its leaf does not wither;
> And in whatever he does, he prospers.
> The wicked are not so,
> But they are like chaff which the wind drives away.
> Therefore the wicked will not stand in the judgment,
> Nor sinners in the assembly of the righteous.
> For the Lord knows the way of the righteous,
> But the way of the wicked will perish. (NASB)

When Christ is at the center, the distinct roles that we assume have allowed us to claim unity in Christian heritage (by understanding the origin of the family as outlined in the first three chapters of Genesis and in the catechism questions that ask: "Who made you?" [God]; "Of what were you made?" [Of dust]; "What doth that teach you?" [To be humble and mindful of death]). Even without the experiential wisdom of a Christian history or practice in our families of origin, Kent and I claim a Christian heritage through Christ's redemption. That is, we know that no one is naturally "born into" the family of God. Being "born again" is the equal footing that we all need. Adoption is not just a Christian metaphor or the process by which we became parents: adoption into Christianity is the process by which we claim our heritage.

One of the texts commonly used by members of our denomination for family Bible study is the *Westminster Shorter Catechism*. It was written for lay people (technically, "babes and imbeciles"!) in the 1640s by an assembly called the Westminster Divines, a group of pastors who also assembled the *Westminster Confession of Faith* and the *Westminster Larger Catechism*. These three texts together offer the central teachings of the Reformation. The *Shorter Catechism* offers 107 questions on the following subjects: God as Creator (questions 1-12); Original Sin (questions 13-20); Christ the Redeemer (questions 21-38); The Ten Commandments (questions 39-84); the Sacraments of Baptism and Holy Communion (questions 85-97); and the Lord's Prayer (questions 98-107).

The *Shorter Catechism* question number 34 addresses what it means to be a "born again" Christian. This *Shorter Catechism* question defines our born-again status as adoption:

Question: What is Adoption?
Answer: Adoption is an act of God's free grace, whereby we are received into the number, and have a right to all of the privileges of the sons of God.

We also see this outlined in the Bible, in Galatians 4:7: "Therefore, you're no longer a slave (orphan), but a son; and if a son, then an heir through God."

When Christ is at the center, the distinct roles that we assume have allowed us to claim a unity in family purpose. Kent is called to be a pastor and with his call come special and unique expectations upon me, his wife. When Christ is at the center, we have been able to embrace our dual call with a sense of shared obedience to God's word.

When Christ is at the center, the distinct roles that we assume have allowed us to claim a unity in family structure. A family structure designed by foster care and adoption is a unique unit. Later in this chapter I will discuss the distinct miracle of each of our four children's placement in our family and the pain of our one disrupted adoption. One of the distinct challenges that families like ours face is race and a confusion of birth order. Son Knox came to us in May 2003, at five months, having had one foster placement. His adoption was finalized in February 2004. Daughter AJ came to us in April 2004, at fifteen-and-a-half years old, having had eleven previous foster placements. Her adoption was finalized in March 2006. Daughter Mary came to us at one hour old. Son Knox and I got to be present at the hospital at her birth and were privileged to be the first people to hold and touch her. Mary had no foster placements and her adoption was finalized in October 2006. Foster daughter S came to us in 2007 at two days old. At the hospital we signed a "foster to adopt" contract, only to have S removed from our home because the agency's director didn't like the placement coordinator's choice of a "white" home for an African-American child. Son Matt came to us in February 2009 at the age of sixteen; Matt's adoption was finalized in November 2010, with the whole family getting dressed up and going to the courthouse, returning home to a sheet cake the size of a small refrigerator and a great neighborhood celebration.

Even this book that you are reading has been marked by our family. I finished the first chapter after Knox's arrival. AJ came in the midst of chapter two. Mary came during chapter three. S came and was taken from us during the first draft of this chapter. Chapter five and all revisions for publication happened when Matt came home.

Like it or not, ready or not, we enter into the spotlight of inquisition each time we leave our house, as many people want to understand what it is like to be a transracial family or to adopt a teenager. Are those your real children? Are we a real family? Do we feel like real parents? Do our children love us? How can we afford the expense of adoption? Do we trust the bonds created by adoption? Does our extended family accept us? My children are apparently so startling to many people that they figure as aberrations.

One time, Kent was filling a pulpit at a small church in a small town. These places scare me, and for good reason. Knox was asleep on my shoulder and Mary was asleep in the car seat. A man walked up to me, not knowing that I was the preacher's wife, and said: "So, is it chic for white women to adopt black kids these days?" I took a deep breath and stood up to meet his gaze.

"Are you a Christian?" I asked him.

"Yes, ma'am," he replied.

"Did God save you because it was *chic*?" We locked eyes until he dropped his head. He stammered something unintelligible and backed away slowly, seeming to understand that even when the bear does not look like the cubs, the trauma of having one's head ripped off by a protective mama can be bloody business.

When Christ is at the center of our family, the distinct roles that we assume have allowed us to claim a unity in family purpose—even when the rest of the world can't get beyond the transracial picture that we present.

When Christ is at the center of our marriage, our worship refreshes and equips us even as we are in the spotlight Lord's Day after Lord's Day. Kent and I have always had an extensive hospitality ministry. From 2002 to 2007, Kent was a church planter in Purcellville, Va. During the first two years, I was preparing around fifty meals each Lord's Day. The labor involved in this, and the wear and tear on our house and again, privacy, was mind-boggling. Many, many women—some strangers—came up along my side, giving me money, recipes, prayer support, and counsel. My friends from the Syracuse RP Church organized cooking days, sending up truckloads of baked goods and lasagna for our Lord's Day fellowship meals. But even so, this intense hospitality ministry, which overlapped with the placement of five-month-old Knox and fifteen-and-a-half-year-old AJ, was exhausting. Learning to be refreshed in the context of intense labor is important spiritual work. God truly gave us what we needed. When Christ was at the center, we learned to "draft" off God's word the way cyclists draft off of another cyclist during a long race. Perhaps even more importantly, when Christ was at the center, we learned to say no and to close the door.

When Christ is at the center of our marriage, our work outside of the home—our service in the community—is conducted with relevance, integrity, and courage. Both in organized service (for example, planning a vacation Bible school and hosting more children for VBS than we have church members) and unplanned service (for example, hosting children in my neighborhood for play dates, preschool, knitting class, and meals during snow days and sick days) has allowed us to fulfill God's simple directive to care for others.

When Christ is at the center of our marriage, we have been able to maintain a Christian household that ministers to others. When Christ is not at the center, all of our good intentions are swallowed up by selfishness.

How do we put Christ at the center? By intentionally holding all things captive to Christ, each moment of each day. By never daring to do anything without fervent prayer, seeking the Lord's wisdom, counsel, blessing, and life-sustaining breath. I learned, during those years, that the idea that one is ever too busy to pray is delusion of the most dangerous variety.

In our first year of ministry, we remained in Beaver Falls. Kent served as pastoral intern for the Geneva Church, working under Pastor Bruce Backensto and the elders there. I stopped teaching and started to recover from the previous two years of Christian life. Only Kent knew how badly I needed to step out of the public and into the home. Kent and I wanted to start a family (through adoption or birth) and I needed to learn how to shift gears. In our first year of marriage, I rested, regrouped, and recovered from my painful conversion. In our first year of marriage, in the context of normal Christian family life, Kent and I developed our philosophy of hospitality and of mercy ministry.

Two distinct kinds of home-based ministry developed in our first year of marriage: ministry to those who know God (encouraging the fellowship of the saints through hospitality) and ministry to those who do not yet know God (developing a theology of the public, meeting the "stranger at the gate," and finding intentional ways and means to bring the gospel to the outcast, the lost, and the lonely). At different times over the years we have had to emphasize one ministry community over the other. For my personality, it was always much easier to meet the outcast at the gate and bring her home. I love first gospel contacts. I love the raw and risky conversations and relationships that develop from this.

After spending the 2001–2002 year in Beaver Falls, Kent was called by the Trinity RPC of Beltsville, Md., to plant a church in Northern Virginia. With our two cats and one dog, we packed our U-Haul and moved to Purcellville, Va., a small Northern Virginia suburb outside of Washington, D.C. Church planting is lonely work. A church plant is considered a daughter church, a minor child who will thrive under the protection, support, guidance, and encouragement of the mother church. Our daughter church started to look stillborn almost before we unpacked the U-Haul.

First, our "seed family," the family who chooses to labor with the pastor to bring the daughter church into adulthood, abandoned not just the church plant but the denomination—before we even arrived on site! They helped us move in and told us they were splitting. They told us that they decided that God was in fact *not* calling them to plant a church. Since they heard this call from God between the time that they recruited us to accept the job offer and the time when we pulled the U-Haul into the driveway, it might have been helpful had they alerted us to God's (perceived) proclamation. What was the reason that God told them to not unite with the church plant? They didn't want to "lack fellowship."

All that being said, Kent and I arrived in Purcellville in April 2002 with no seed family and no ministry community who had any inkling we had arrived. We trusted that God doesn't get addresses wrong and that God had us where he wanted us. We just wondered why.

Purcellville, Va., is a small (but growing) and wealthy outer D.C. suburb. It is located in Loudoun County, the fastest growing and wealthiest county in the U.S. The average income here is twice my husband's paycheck, and first-year public high school teachers in our county have a higher starting salary than tenured and senior professors make at Syracuse University. Why are we here? This is what we asked the Lord on our first night in our new home.

The first manifestation of this church plant (2002–2004) was exclusively a college ministry. A small Christian college courting the homeschool community had just opened its doors, right across the street from our house. Students flocked to our services, our Bible studies, and mostly our home, in droves. For two years our church consisted of 35-40 college students, two local families, and the Butterfields. At this time, many other families, one at a time, visited for a while. Each left after a month, using the same reason that our original seed family gave to us: they lacked fellowship and they feared for their children in a church without other like-minded families.

Over the years, I have contemplated what this really means. What does it really mean to "lack fellowship"? At least as it regards the handful of families that showed immediate excitement and then after a month a changed heart, this is what "lacking fellowship" means. It means that the family needs to be in a church made up of people who are just like they, who raise their children using the same childrearing methods, who take the same stance on birth control, schooling, voting, breastfeeding, dress codes, white flour, white sugar, gluten, childhood immunizations, the observance of secular and religious holidays. We encountered families who feared diversity with a primal fear. They often told us that they didn't want to "confuse" their children by exposing them to differences in parenting standards among Christians. I suspect that they feared that deviation from their rules might provide a window for children to see how truly diverse the world is and that temptation might lead them astray. Over and over and over again I have heard this line of thinking from the fearful and the faith-struggling. We in the church tend to be more fearful of the (perceived) sin in the world than of the sin in our own hearts. Why is that?

Here is what I think. I believe that there is no greater enemy to vital life-breathing faith than insisting on cultural sameness. When fear rules your theology, God is nowhere to be found in your paradigm, no matter how many Bible verses you tack onto it. I think that as parents we would be more effective in our parenting if we leveled with our children, if we told them that some of our dearly held rules are not morally grounded but are made for our convenience. I know that many times when I insist that my children turn off the video, my "rules" are the result of my own noise-sensitivity, not some moral abhorrence about Pixar or Disney. I never know how to respond to the women who tell me that they need to be in a church made of people with whom they can identify, people who are like them.

This upstart college with whom we ironically held a shared community had no health clinic, limited dining hall services on Sunday, and no women's dean. I was driving women students to doctor's appointments (and learning how to give subcutaneous injections), counseling more students than I could have imagined, leading two Bible studies per week, and still serving endless meals every Lord's Day. These students were amazing. I genuinely loved these students and learned much from them about grace and perseverance. These students were smart and devout in their faith. They also were sheltered. They imparted to me in a first-hand way the serious dangers of isolating our children from real life. Adult children can appear obedient when they are tuning out instead of acting out. College life tends to bring out all the fears and doubts and perceptions of contradictions and hypocrisies. Between this hyper-sensitivity to authority and rules, and a growing sexual awareness, we met students who were struggling with real moral issues. Their unsuspecting parents had no idea how their over-protection had dangerously ill-prepared their beloved, overly protected children from all of this. Sin—especially sexual sin—has a sneaky way of triumphing in an environment of secrecy and shame. Kent and I had our ministry cut out for us.

What was most amazing about those days in the church plant was how labor-intensive it was. No life experience or professional training had prepared me for this labor. The hospitality demands on the Lord's Day and throughout the week were daunting. So many meals to prepare. So much preparation and cleanup. So many trips to Costco for supplies. So many unexpected knocks on the door. Students came for breakfast and stayed late into the night. Our work was always different. Kent would go from teaching large groups of students the doctrine and theology of applied Christian living, taking other students to the local nursing home to pray with and for the residents, helping students with papers and homework, to teaching some kids how to drive a car. The wear and tear on our house, car, washing machine, and bodies was enormous. We worshiped at this time in a gymnasium at a local community center. Saturday night before the community center closed, the gymnasium was open to the public for pick-up basketball games. Custodial service for the community center was not in place until Monday morning. At one point, my first task each Lord's Day was to clean the public restrooms in the community center so that they were presentable for our church community.

Our church life never lacked for love. We never "lacked fellowship." I still laugh to think that families left us because they thought we "lacked fellowship." We had more fellowship than we knew what to do with! Real fellowship requires stepping outside of you, and our church community stretched us and enriched us.

We cared for the students as faithfully as we could and they cared for us in return. We were sustained by their prayers. They helped us in material ways, as well. We never lacked for house-sitters, dog-walkers, lawn-mowers, leaf-rakers. Each year they faithfully and generously remembered our anniversary. We were privileged to see a whole generation of students through college and into graduate school or marriage. Kent even had the privilege of baptizing the baby of one such couple.

Our mother church, Trinity RPC, provided us with a generous hospitality budget. Pastor Steve and Julie Bradley came out as many times as they could to help us with the after-service studies and activities. Elder TG and family faithfully came out many Lord's Days, bringing food and encouragement and helping hands and hearts. One family even drove all the way from Pennsylvania once a month and contributed bountifully to our worship, meals, psalm singing, and fellowship. Our beloved dentist and his family worshiped regularly with us for over two years even though they hold strong doctrinal ties in Baptist theology. And a strong handful of parents of our college ministry came to our aid. These families gave to us the counsel that we desperately needed at this time. They sustained us with their prayers and with material help.

Each week, I benefited from the recipes that many women gave to me. Sue Wilkey's "Groundhog Day Soup" was on the menu each week, as was NM's minestrone, Floy Smith's oat bread, Robyn Zorn's chocolate chip cookies, and my own Mediterranean chicken. The *More with Less* cookbook was my constant companion. My mother kept me flush in cooking magazines and gadgets. When she and my stepfather would visit, she would stock my freezer with homemade meatballs and *pasta e fagiole*. One year she bought me the top-of-the-line Kitchen Aid with all the attachments. I still use it almost every day.

Then something started to slip. We started to notice something about our college ministry. It was always very busy, very active, very exciting, but it never really took root. Students were great at bringing other students, but they were awkward in talking with people outside of their world. Sometimes, they were so busy sharpening their intellectual sword that they lacked compassion and empathy for people who didn't already share their worldview.

One time, on a Saturday, a young college woman, S, was baking cookies with me. A neighbor came by at the same time to return a book and mentioned something to me about her daughter trying out for something at the local public high school. The neighbor was sharing a concern that she had about something going on in the high school, something that her special needs daughter would not understand. S shook her head and muttered audibly, "Sending a child to the public schools is like giving pearls to the swine." This student was not known to be combative or rude. She was so accustomed to being around like-minded people that she slipped. I know that she did not intend to do harm. But her heart was revealed in this slip (as our hearts always are). My neighbor was, understandably, offended, and, privately, the following week, said to me that she knew the student was hurling the Bible at her, but she had no idea what it meant: Was she the pearl or the pig? Why did this pert and disrespectful girl think that public schools were for the pigs? These sorts of encounters happened too frequently. Of course, these sorts of encounters can provide wonderful teachable moments, but to convert them into these takes a skill and grace that I lacked. I felt broken. My unsaved neighbor needed Jesus more than this college student needed to hurl a few well-rehearsed epithets about the evils of public schools.

One day while I was scrubbing a coffee stain from our beige carpet it dawned on me: I am now caring for the very people I would have given anything to study just a few years back. And then with the same flash of insight, I wondered if this really was what God was calling me to do. Of course, knowing God's call is very humbling business. How do we really know the difference between "God's call" and our own selfish desires? I personally confuse the two all the time. At the same time, Kent and I had completed the lengthy program of study and home study process to be adoptive parents. We knew that our current ministry could not sustain a household with children. It lacked the appropriate boundaries for parenting. Desiring children can be a noble pursuit, but if it's not God's will then it is simply a more sanctified form of covetousness. So I scrubbed at the stain in my carpet and tried to focus on the ministry that God had given me.

Then two phone calls came that would change our lives forever. I remember someone telling me that God doesn't act quickly, he acts suddenly. We had been licensed to adopt a child for six months. And within one day we were matched with four children: a five-and-a-half-month baby boy through a private Christian adoption agency and a sibling group of three from the public welfare system. While this did not seem quick (we had been trying to start a family from the beginning of our marriage), it sure was sudden. And now we had a fateful choice before us: the infant or the sibling group? We had twelve hours to decide.

Adoption is a complex affair, especially when you have to choose between children and agencies. Adoption has a complex political and financial underside. In the U.S., the average cost of private adoption is $25,000 (*Adoptive Families Magazine*, Feb. 2006). Because of the culture of legalized abortion and the exoneration of teenage pregnancy, infants are rarely available for adoption. Adoption also suffers from bad press, with all members of the adoption triangle (children, birth parents, and adoptive parents) suffering from misrepresentation. We were surprised and horrified to learn that even Christian crisis pregnancy centers encourage teenagers to try to parent their children rather than consider the adoption alternative. Also, because of these social factors, the children who end up in the foster care system are often trapped for years and years, as social workers try to patch the holes of sin and poverty that render bad parents abusers or worse. Trapped with these children are identities forged by trauma, neglect, self-hatred, and the degradation of drugs and poverty.

Birth parents who gravitate toward private adoption generally relinquish their own parental rights. Birth parents who choose private adoption usually know their limits and receive the counsel and support that they need to come to this painful and sacrificial decision. Children in the foster care system have birth parents who do not know their limits. They try to parent beyond their means. Some are criminally neglectful and abusive; others are mentally ill or themselves victims of prisons of poverty, abuse, neglect, drugs, and dysfunction. The parental rights of birth parents whose children end up in foster care are usually terminated by a judge, a process that requires documentation over time of abuse or neglect. This lengthy and invasive process can eat up whole childhoods. It costs a lot of money to adopt a child through a private agency and it is "free" to adopt a child from the public welfare system. At the same time, the moral and fiscal cost of retaining a person in the foster care system for a lifetime is enormous. The question isn't *if* any of us pay for the cost of orphanhood but *when*—and with what kind of hope left over at the end.

Kent and I have never been the type of people who believed that only babies are worthy to adopt. We know that all children need loving and stable homes. As people converted outside of covenant homes, we know firsthand that the covenant isn't only for babies born to biological believers. Yes, the first three years of life are formative and the opportunity to parent a child from infancy into adulthood is a privilege. But, life is precious and children beloved not because they may heal and grow, but because God made us in his image. If that is good enough for God, it must be good enough for us.

When two phone calls came in the same day from two different agencies, we had to choose: the baby or the brother and sisters? How does one choose?

It is times like this that I am grateful that I am a Reformed Christian. I know that I don't choose. God chooses. He rules and he overrules. We walk in faith and (at times) terror, but we walk nonetheless. Our walk into parenthood led to the next phase of our life.

Our beloved son Knox, our beautiful five-month-old baby boy, created before the foundations of the world and destined by God to be a Butterfield, joined us three days after our second anniversary, May 22, 2003. His skin is mocha, just like rich dark coffee with the perfect amount of cream. I loved him immediately with a love I didn't know existed. He had lost so much by the time that I met him: he had lost a birth mother and a foster mother. My only care at the time was to get to know him and to assure him that I would be there for him no matter what. I "wore" him in a sling, like African mothers do. Together we walked, worked, slept, heart-to-heart. He bonded, slowly at first and then with his whole heart. During our early days, as he cried my own heart cried for the sibling group who was not with us. I was overrun with emotion and with a sense of my own inadequacy.

AJ came next, 11 months later, at the age of fifteen-and-a-half, in April 2004. We were her eleventh foster home. For AJ, I stand in a long, long line of bad mothers. Kent stands alone in the role of a father. And although he tried beyond measure to take an active role in her life, because of the history that preceded him, he was rooted in a role enshrined in absence and mystery. I loved AJ immediately and wanted to champion her cause. With Knox, my most important task was bonding. With AJ, my most important task was recognition—the ability to see her and to try to understand.

The values and social arrangements of a privileged family life too often regard teenagers in the foster care system as invisible or dangerous. AJ taught me (and continues to teach me) the value of recognizing, of looking and seeing a person with eyes of intimacy. There is a moment in parenting an older child when you feel that "click" of recognition, when you swap the lack of shared life experience for a simple love. This happened for me when I was picking AJ up from school during the first week that she lived with us. Knox and I sat in the car in a long line of families waiting to pick up their teenage child. I felt an awful fear that I would not recognize AJ. I had just met her five days ago. Had I really looked at her? Had I spent the time required to know my child? No. I hadn't and not one of the ten rejecting mothers who preceded me had. As I sat amidst a sea of strange faces, I felt the weight of our collective neglect. I started to panic, trying to recall to mind the color T-shirt she was wearing. What if I lost her? What if she ran away? With great relief, I found her. Always poised, even in the most stressful situations, there was AJ standing at ease with a group of girls waiting casually for their mothers to pick them up. Once my eyes held her I didn't want to let go. AJ reminds me that too often our lofty goals for our children interfere with simply recognizing them. AJ does not live in our home any longer. Our lifestyles and values clashed too deeply. AJ fears discipline the way a fish fears dry land. But we talk and visit and hold on to our fragile relationship.

Mary came eighteen months later, as a newborn, in November 2005. Amy Comin, Doug's wife, called in October to tell us that four biracial or African-American babies were soon to be born to a small private adoption agency with no waiting families. I called the number that Amy gave to me immediately and by God's providence, the agency's director took my phone call even though I was from out of state. Out-of-state adoptions in the U.S. are even more complex because of the need to gain approval from social workers and attorneys in each state. Many agencies are reluctant to even consider out-of-state adoptions. (This is part of why many adoptive parents prefer international adoptions.) But God forged the path for Mary's adoption. Indeed, I had the privilege to hold her during her first hour of life. In that hour, I sang to her Psalm 104 (Knox calls this the "Butterfield Baby Song") and she queued my voice immediately. She taught me the marvelous ways that newborns learn to trust and grow. She teaches me the iron behind trust and the powerful strides the human brain stakes out in infancy and childhood. I watch her step into the world with a confidence that still startles me. She knows something that the rest of my children don't: that it is safe to take her family for granted.

S came fourteen months later, as a newborn, in January 2007. With S, we faced our first disrupted adoption. Her adoption disrupted after she was in our care for ten days. The director was on vacation when the placement coordinator placed a black child in a white home. That really rocked her world. How can people who don't match be a family? With her racism on the front line, she refused to support the adoption. We witnessed racism firsthand: we watched a racist community (Department of Family Services) "solve" the problem of race (black kids who don't match white parents) by putting into place a racist solution (disrupt the adoption). When S's adoption started to unravel, we were faced with the moral question: Do we fight this or concede? We did neither. Instead, we prayed. We at first prayed lofty, conceited prayers, trying to force God's hand. Then, after we got sick of our own pride interfering with God's work, we whittled down the prayer to this: a covenant family for this dear child that I hold in my arms, because Your arms, dear Lord, shaped and formed her, and Your arms are the ones that will always hold this dear child, not mine, but yours. The Department of Family Services called with a date to remove this baby in my arms from our home. It was heartbreaking. We felt powerless and wondered if we had done the right thing by not fighting this battle. One of the hardest facets of adoption is the total exposure the adoptive family feels as the agency or birth mother selects or rejects you. What does rejection say about us as people? As a family? Am I right to believe that segregation (placing children of color with families of color) is not the solution to racism? Do I believe that to the harm of my four biracial children and in defense alone of my white privilege? Am I right or wrong, good or bad, competent or incompetent? Will my family stand the test of time?

We had two Christian attorneys who were willing to take the agency to court, since it is illegal to use race to disrupt an adoptive placement. (MEPA—the 1994 Multiethnic Placement Act—is the antidiscrimination law that prohibits this as well as racial matching as the primary placement criterion.) But we did not want S to suffer as a victim of the court system, a situation that could have retained her in foster care for years. We believe that we adopt children because of need. We reasoned like this: if there is no need, there is no adoption. We reminded ourselves that we are not called to covet other people's children. But we also knew from firsthand experience, having adopted before through the public welfare system, that this agency is no friend to children. Like other government agencies, it is overburdened and understaffed. Children do fall through the cracks. We didn't want this for S. We were torn and in doubt. Kent posted a prayer request on our denomination's prayer list—"Covie- net." Our denomination is a praying community. I believe that there were thousands of saints praying for this child on the day that Kent posted our plea. Kent's request was simple: Dear God, may S have a Christian home.

The day that was S's last one with us was a dark and fearful one. Did we make the wrong decision? Wouldn't we have fought to retain the other children in our home? We tearfully brought S back to the agency and there we met S's preferred potential adoptive family. They are African American and they are Christian. God heard our prayers. Yes, we were hurt. Deeply. But S wasn't! In God's amazing mercy, he used us to protect the baby! Isn't that at the center of our prayers for our children? He didn't hurt us to punish us. We were hurt in service to him. Why was S with us for ten days? What kind of spiritual warfare played out in the hidden backdrop of those ten days? Did our humble prayers shake the gates of heaven for this orphan child? Did our prayers avail much? Did God use our prayers to secure for her a Christian home? The day that the agency took S away, we found on our porch an expansive take-out bag from the restaurant *Red, Hot, and Blue* (including my favorite, banana pudding) and this note, scribbled in pencil, with a child's drawing of a flower with a petal falling off. The note read:

> A family that never opens its heart never feels heartbroken. A family that never welcomes in others never misses them when they leave. A family that never embraces life's risks, never really lives. Thinking of you all on this tough day. With love from the many, many people whose lives you've touched and who love you all.

I don't know who penned the note or drew the picture. But the note captures for me an often overlooked spiritual truth: Betrayal and risk are at the heart of the gospel life. This I know: God heard my prayers.

In this broken world, people break promises (and contracts). The social worker that made the contract and the social worker that broke the contract are women I respect and value. We come to the table with different points of view. Because we are Christ's, we know that children are not grafted into a family to resolve our fertility problems or to boost our egos or to complete our family pictures or because we match color or race or nation-status. We know, because we are Christ's, that adoption is a miracle. In a spiritual sense, it is the miracle at the center of the Christian life. We who are adopted by God are those given a new heart, a "rebirth."

When God brings children out of neglect, abuse, dysfunction, gangs, drugs, and hate, and places them in a covenant home, he has just moved a mountain in the hearts and families of men. When God gives a childless couple a child of any age using the means of his powerful will, he has just moved a mountain in the hearts and families of men. When mountains move, the earth shakes. When you stand as close as we have to real-life miracles, you will get roughed up. Mountains are big and we are small. A moving mountain can crush us. Splinters fall from the cross. They travel a long distance and they pierce the skin—maybe even the heart. And wrapped in this risk and danger are God's embrace and promise to work all things (even evil ones) to the good of those who love him. When we read in the book of Romans, "And we know that God causes all things to work together for good to those who love God, to those who are the called according to his purpose" (8:28), we are not to be Pollyanna about this. Many of the "things" we will face come with the razor edges of a fallen and broken world. You can't play poker with God's mercy—if you want the sweet mercy then you must also swallow the bitter mercy. And what is the difference between sweet and bitter? Only this: your critical perspective, your worldview. One of God's greatest gifts is the ability to see and appreciate the world from points of view foreign to your own, points of view that exceed your personal experience. That is what it means to me to grow in Christ—to exceed myself as I stretch to him. The loss of S taught us this.

I think a lot about the way our family had shaped our little church plant. I was our church's precentor (the person who leads the singing). In our denomination, precentors lead by voice and music-director hand motions to indicate the pace of the psalm. During the life of the church plant, I was honored to lead the singing in our church with one and sometimes two children in tow, one in a baby sling and the other on my hip. Knox took great interest as a baby in "helping" me to lead the psalms, swinging his hands to keep the beat or turning the pages of the psalter with arbitrary confidence. Daughter Mary was more dancer than singer, or so it seemed. She kicked her legs and threw her body around or sometimes in the middle of a stanza would fall into a deep sleep. I led the singing of the psalms with my babies attached. My babies often shifted their weight or kicked me in the gut as I precented. It made me think about the "Psalms of Ascent," imagining the Israelites walking as they sang into foreign lands, in weakness and in faith. With babies attached, I felt a sensible and tangible awareness growing in me, a little window into the mystery of the Christian life.

Children bring other children. The children in our home brought other children into our home. When we became parents, we suddenly became a children's church. Because we are licensed foster parents, we had access to children who don't have homes (and live in group homes). We have enjoyed vital and vibrant ministries that emerge in the process of daily life: knitting club for the girls on the block (with the *Westminster Shorter Catechism* taught alongside knit and purl), pick-up football for the four-year-old boys (with prayer and snacks to follow), and neighborhood preschool. We also enjoyed the lost art of simply being available to care for children lost in emergencies, from snow days that strand children at home and send parents to work, to domestic abuse or worse. We see this as an investment in community. Anything worth doing will take time and cost you something. We noticed, as our attention focused more on families and children, that many people in our community protect themselves from inconvenience as though inconvenience is deadly. We have decided that we are not inconvenienced by inconvenience. The needs of children come up unexpectedly. We are sure that the Good Samaritan had other plans that fateful day. Our plans are not sacred. Our house is open to children for after-school care. No money is exchanged. The younger children enjoy the attention of the older children and we enjoy seeing a small shadow of real community emerge— right here in our kitchen.

My attention for the college ministry weakened over time as my interest and commitment to children (those that God would allow us to adopt and those who remain trapped in the foster care system) increased. Parenting adopted children and children marked by the trauma of foster care is serious business. Adoption is not a pathology that marks and plagues people and families for their whole life. But adoption is a complex, paradoxical event that combines loss, brokenness, and rejection with gain, connection, and embrace. No child asks to be adopted. No child asks for incompetent or rejecting birth parents. No child asks to be constantly told how "lucky" he is to be adopted. Wanted or not, adoption always starts with loss. Adoption always combines ambiguous loss with unrequested gain. An adopted child faces this paradox—this ambiguous grief—at each developmental stage. His or her family must choose to either welcome the complexity or make the child go it alone. We choose to walk alongside our children, even as we don't always understand how deep or how raw the complexity rests. This journey is frightful. At its core is this: do I love Jesus enough to face my children's potential rejection of me?

I began to grow weary and tired of the issues that the women brought into my home from the campus. I started to feel like all I was doing was helping homeschool loyalists choose between their parachurch allegiances. As I faced the demons of neglect and loss and the hard work of extra care and nurture, I found myself constantly out of step with women who were my peers. And the crowning moment for me was when the mother of one of my favorite students said to me, "Rosaria, I don't understand how a Christian can be effective in parenting foster children. As I see it, if you can't homeschool them and you can't spank them, you surely can't lead them to Jesus."

This woman—this friend of mine—did not say this with intended malice or disrespect. It merely came from her heart and from the narrow walls of a fear-driven theology. It came from an odd allegiance to the means of discipline and love rather than its purpose or origin. From our experience, children in the welfare state are no less worthy of a covenant home than the biological children of believers. God calls us to discipline our children in an effective way. Spanking is not the only means of discipline, and for children who have been abused it is the least effective means. And while children in the foster care system are wards of the state, we have found that social workers are willing to take into consideration alternative means of schooling. We have homeschooled a child in foster care. We firmly believed that it was her only hope—and we were successful in convincing her social workers and public school teachers and guidance counselors of this. We were successful in accomplishing the educational and social goals that we had for her in the year that we were given permission to educate her at home.

Indeed, my own experience as a foster parent has made me a great advocate of homeschooling—but not for the reasons that most homeschool loyalists provide. I have found that traditional school settings are hostile to children who live under constant stress and duress. I resent the idea that, just because it is "free," public education is the first choice. Public education is one choice among many, but it is not the norm against which other schooling options are to be graded.

For about a year, a sixteen-year-old girl named Jessica came to our church and home. She was in terminal foster care and lived in a local group home. She was saddled with labels, mental illness categories, and medication. She helped me with VBS and with crocheting granny squares for blankets. Like most children in terminal foster care, she fell between the cracks of the system when she turned eighteen. In our first-floor restroom, the children stand on a stool to wash their hands that Jessica made in a woodworking class in an adult psychiatric ward. One day in church, Pastor Steve Bradley was preaching on knowing God's call. Jessica was listening with rapt attention. After the service, she approached Pastor Steve and said, "Steve, I hear voices all the time. How do I know the difference between hearing the voice of God and hearing the voices of my own sick mind?" With great compassion, Pastor Steve said, "Dear one, we all have to check the voices of our own sick mind with the Bible. Daily. You are no different." I have always been so grateful that my church is a safe place for the orphans and the outcasts—for God's children.

Jessica told me later that day that never before had someone made her feel so good. It was so good to know that, at least in regards to this, she was no different. It gave her great comfort to know that others struggled, too.

When she turned eighteen, we watched first-hand the graphic horror faced by children who "age out" of foster care. In some Orwellian, grotesque turn of phrase, the welfare state calls this "aging out" process (i.e., turning eighteen) "emancipation." Here is what happened to Jessica. On her eighteenth birthday, she was moved from a group home for children with mental illness to a series of adult psychiatric wards, first in Maryland, then Connecticut, then New York. We lost her when she left Maryland. In 2010, a month before Matt's adoption was finalized, we learned that Jessica died in a homeless shelter in New York on her twenty-third birthday.

Jessica was a child of God.

She spent time in our home.

She wanted to be adopted.

She never was.

She died alone.

In November 2010, at Matt's adoption ceremony at the Loudoun County Courthouse, I was privileged to read to the court a short text about what adoption means. I looked out at a sea of faces, children of all ages and races and abilities, parents and siblings in our best dress; I felt peaceful gratitude that the Lord had put Matt in our family. But in the backdrop of this picture, in the crevice behind the blessing offered to us by these children who will forever be our emotional betters, whom we need more than they need us, I could picture, thick as pudding, the faces of the absent, lost, dead, unnamed, unknown.

I will always regard Jessica as the child we did not adopt.

The college students who remained with us after the children and foster children started coming became our allies in real outreach ministry. We all grew in Christ in our opportunity to serve people who would otherwise be invisible to us because of our privilege or fear. G was our advocate even after he graduated and moved away. B moved into our basement for a summer and became daughter AJ's confidante and swim partner. D moved to Maryland after graduation and tied in with the Trinity church. Others married and stayed in the community for a while.

All of this bounty came from God's blessing upon my marriage to Kent. My mom and stepfather love Kent. I love Kent's sisters, brothers-in-law, and nephews. Someone once teased that, in our family, we have enough PhDs and differences of political opinions to become our own small unaccredited liberal arts college! During one fellowship dinner at our house, we had Kent's family in attendance. One of the students, excited to have a whole room full of PhDs, asked what advice we had for him in his pursuit of his doctorate. Kent's oldest sister, Rebecca, challenged him — and the rest of us — to recite our theses in one sentence. We all sounded like such idiots, all except for Rebecca. Her PhD is in Environmental Studies, and her thesis could be reduced to this: "Dead trees don't grow." Well, she won the "name that thesis in four notes" contest hands down!

I never was a seasoned pastor's wife. We were church planters, and that is scrappy work. But I believe, from my limited experience, that there is a little-known secret about the inner spiritual lives of pastor's wives: The experience of really knowing the man behind the pulpit, counting the costs of his week, palpably know-ing how deeply Satan wants the gospel to simply die from lack of interest, and seeing the Holy Spirit triumph in his preaching even when just the hour before all looked grim, is a great shot in the arm to enduring faith. I wish that others knew this: Pastor's wives get the cream of the ministry, even as we sacrifice certain aspects of our personal, private, and family lives to have this. I have found my life as Kent's wife to be full, rich, amusing, edifying, and exciting. I have tasted a small bit of the gospel of Jesus Christ. I would not trade this life for anything.

In 2007, we closed the church plant. We were holding services in Harpers Ferry, W. Va., at the time of the last worship service. Kent preached to a packed crowd. Friends came from Pennsyl-vania and Maryland. Kent delivered a resounding sermon about thanking God at all times, not only when we win. I was in the back, tears welling in my eyes, when the doors opened and people I vaguely recognized but could not place walked into the service. A beautiful family with a year-old baby girl approached me. I shifted Mary to one hip and the woman put the other baby in my arms. "Rosaria, here is our baby. We came to worship with you today." Baby S, taken away from us, and returned briefly on this fateful day. Baby S's dad is a jolly, joyful man, whose large mocha hands warm a wide expanse. He scooped Knox into his lap and told him all about how God used him to help Baby S when she was so tiny. He told Knox that we are one, big, Christian family. It was time, and, without thinking, I took both Mary and Baby S with me to the front of the church to lead in the singing of Psalm 78. Kent was reading from the book of Exodus. He was retelling the story of Moses' parents placing him in a basket of reeds, lowering him into the Nile, not knowing his destination. I handed Kent Baby S, as I flipped through the psalter and fished in my pocket for my pitch pipe. Kent embraced the baby in his arms, and mouthed, "Who is this?"

I told him, and he broke into tears.

5

Homeschooling and Middle Age

Purcellville, Va., 2012

I write these days as a drowning person gulps air. I steal time here and there, and in the backdrop of my theft you will find children, friends of children, and a husband whose government job and its constant din of stress and competition organize our days. We have a minivan that Kent has christened the Traveling Garbage Can. I have been known to clean out this van by sending in my trusty Golden Retriever, Sally, to fetch old PB&J sandwiches, juice boxes, and pizza crusts. Sally is the same age as my youngest daughter; it was like having twins separated by species. Sally was housebroken with then-three-year-old Knox, because, in my world, that is what summer and backyards are for. My dear, old dog Murphy is buried in the backyard, under our butterfly garden. Last year, I planted forty-five basil plants there; they thrived until a woodchuck (an Italian one, for sure) ate his way through the crop.

We are a typical classically educated homeschool family. As I write this sentence, three of our four children live at home. My eighteen-year-old son just returned home from work. Matt is a service technician at a local auto place. He will vigilantly and unsuccessfully attempt to scrub the grime off his hands in preparation for the annual Firefighter Banquet tonight. Matt is a volunteer firefighter. Our house is less than a mile from the station, which means that, as one of the senior firefighters now, he is on call a lot. He loves to serve and to take care of people.

He studies anatomy (for EMT work), mechanics, and fire science. He and I share the Traveling Garbage Can. When he takes the van to the banquet tonight, he will remember without my asking to take out the children's car seats and leave them in the hallway, just in case. He is careful and vigilant in his protection of our family.

While Matt is upstairs showering, Knox and Mary are outside looking for signs of spring. It seems a little early for this, as a light February snow is also falling. But this morning Knox spotted the first male robin of the season, here scouring for housing for his family. As I write now, a Sign of Spring flops on my writing desk, five inches from my right wrist. The First Worm. He will keep me company for a while and then we will return him to a more accommodating habitat. Like it or not, the Geneva Convention comes to all bug cages and traps at the Butterfields' before we wash up for dinner.

We love to study God's natural world. Last fall, the children and I attended a fascinating lecture on bat echo-location (a bat's ability to "track" by inaudible sound). When Mary started to tank at about 8:30 p.m., I leaned over and whispered to Knox, "We have to go."

Incredulous, he whispered back, "Aw, Mom, it is getting so interesting! I know half of the people in this room. Can't someone else drive me home?"

"No, dear. You still need a car seat and are too young to be getting home at 10:30 p.m."

We study science in formal ways, by attending lectures on a variety of subjects, such as bat echo-location and amphibian monitoring, but we also study science in the same way that we jam together in music (piano, guitar, tin whistle, pots and pans, handmade trilling frog wood instruments, etc.). When Mary was two, I had to check her pockets before putting her down for naps; she loved to collect wooly bears and stuff them in her pocket for safe keeping. By four she knew how to examine treasures under the microscope, which, in the spring and summer, resides in the kitchen right next to the Kitchen Aid. Mary recently observed that, under the microscope, frog eggs looked like the surface of the moon and the gunk that prodigiously escapes from our cat Big Guy's ears looks like Mount McKinley. At five, she participated in her first amphibian monitoring class (three hours in the classroom; three hours in the field). Her gentle hands allowed her to collect water samples and observe the presence of fairy shrimp without doing them any harm.

Spring is often a treacherous time in my kitchen. Like most homeschool kitchens, mine also serves as a laboratory. Last year, our first sign of spring was three American toads, which Knox carried in to me with great joy and pride. He was covered in mud, and the dogs followed, paw pads thwumping at each step, like sponges releasing muddy water with each joyful bound. (There is a reason that we have almost no carpet in our house. I like Pergo—or any surface to which I can take white vinegar and a garden hose for a wash down.) But the toads! Ah! An unmistakable sign of spring! I quickly covered the pot of minestrone on the stove before admiring Knox's treasure; I still prefer a vegetarian meal at supper.

Knox is older, so he likes to study his treasures differently. He has at least four field guides with him at all times. He is smitten by John Audubon's autobiography, especially the part about his study of migration. Here is the story as Knox loves to tell it: When John was a boy of Knox's age, all he wanted to do was study birds. He studied them, drew them, and collected dead ones. Through this observation, he discovered that birds migrate; this discovery proved Aristotle wrong! Aristotle believed that birds hibernate. Simply by observing and recording what he observed, John Audubon as a boy proved himself a better scientist than Aristotle.

Knox follows in Audubon's footsteps. We have a collection of dead things in the freezer, for dissection and measuring. Recently, an unfortunate Red-eyed Vireo met his unlikely death at our sliding class door. I say "unlikely death" because the finger smudges and the dog nose smutches should have been a giveaway to the flying critter. But, migration is rigorous business. Knox lovingly attempted first aid. When this failed, he studied his specimen. He got out his tools: his Saxon math balance, notebook, pencils (color and number 2), measuring tape, coin box. His specimen weighed 2 pennies and 2 quarters. By his size and color, Knox determined that he was an immature vireo. He placed his specimen in a baggie, marked the baggie with a

Sharpie, and put it in the freezer. Later that day, Kent pulled the specimen out of the freezer, pointed to it, and said, "Not a burrito, right?"

Right.

Learning is risky business.

I tutor in an inspiring homeschool cooperative that uses the curriculum Classical Conversations. Knox and Mary study Latin, geography, English, math, history, science, and fine arts as part of our CC curriculum. They also study piano, ornithology, yoga, and swimming. Our days are full. If the Lord allows, I will turn 50 this year. While I love homeschooling, it isn't always pretty. In Knox's Cub Scout troop last week, a boy asked how homeschool is different from public school. Another boy answered: "At public school, your mom isn't yelling at you." True. Good Point. *Mea culpa*.

There are twin churnings in my house: the daily intellectual excitement (and sometimes frustration) of our rigorous and stimulating homeschool curriculum; and, the hope that the Lord may return Kent to the pulpit ministry. We dream about Kent's return to the pulpit ministry. New church, new homeschool community, new house. Will the boys share a bedroom? Will Grandma, who will move and live with us, keep her hearing aids off as a perpetual act of self-defense? What new birds will we see there? Will we have salamanders in our backyard? Will the Lord use us to build a church, again? Are we ready? Will we fit in—transracial, adopted, Mama's R-rated and scary conversion story, and a few other peculiarities? Nevertheless, there is a spring in our steps, a nervous energy in our house, a bubbling of hope, potential, and possibility. I long to sit under Kent's preaching again.

In 2009, just after Matt joined our household at the age of sixteen, my parents moved from Arizona to Virginia. They did this to help us. They heard the stress in our voices and witnessed the tension in our bodies. Kent loved being a pastor. When the church plant closed in 2007, Kent received a job that required a top security clearance, which in turn allowed him to work on various top-secret government contracts. He went from being a work-from-home pastor-dad to someone juggling one of the highest stress-related jobs in the D.C. area. (Currently, Kent's job objective is "preventing another 9-11.") Money was tight (because expenses were high), and the housing market plummeted so severely that one out of four houses in our county was in foreclosure. My parents, in their late seventies and eighties at the time, moved here with a sense of duty, love, and commitment. They rolled up their sleeves and joined us—full time. My stepfather's Alzheimer's was worsening, and he lost the ability to read (and therefore be connected to the world in his favorite and best way). But he delighted in listening to the children's read-alouds and having others read the *New York Times* to him. He became a night wanderer, though, and dog Sally guarded the front door to keep him safe. Papoo (Greek for Grandpa) died on August 12, 2011. The day before he died, my mom and I heard five-year-old Mary—through the baby monitor in Papoo's room—share the promise of the gospel and the new body and new life promised to him through belief in Jesus.

My mom plays a key role in our homeschool. My mom, at eighty-one, is proficient in Latin, excellent in math, and a trained scientist (medical technologist, by profession). When I accidentally cut off the tip of my pinkie slicing into a farmers' market cantaloupe with a too-sharp knife, my mom shaved off some epithelial cells from my lost chunk of finger to examine on a slide, calling the children over to the microscope with great excitement.

Our world is filled with ideas, hypotheses, field guides, questions, reading, music, and friends. Knox wants to go to Cornell and study ornithology, but knows he needs to get through the third grade first. He participates in bird atlases, bird counts, and environmental work. When the phone rings and a foster child is on the way, Knox is the first to give up his room and his toys. He is a compassionate listener. He is one of the leading "ear" birders in our county. This means that he can identify bird songs faster than people can see them—even distinguishing distress calls from daily ones and accurately identifying birds that intentionally mimic the vocalizations of others. Knox listens to his whole world like this. I asked him once how he could distinguish bird calls, especially during times when the birds' vocalizations sound like a full orchestra. He said, "When you listen to an orchestra, can't you tell the difference between the trumpet and the piano?"

If we move, I will miss our homeschool co-op, neighborhood, and the fellowship that we have in a local church. Our family worships at a local Orthodox Presbyterian Church (OPC). We are members at the Trinity RPC in Beltsville, Md., but its distance makes this an inaccessible church for us. I know this is a touchy subject. I know that many psalm singers hold to the mailman's motto no matter what, declaring neither snow, sleet, rain, blizzard, nor, in our case, Beltway, too treacherous to travail. I believe that a church is a community of believers, and a community serves each other, in sickness and health. Over the years since the church plant closed, we have come to appreciate that a church needs to be in your community, not on your work's commute. (And I know that this is another touchy subject.) The pastor at the OPC is our friend. He is a real friend, which means that, over the years, we have come to appreciate each others' strengths and weaknesses. Real Christian friends are like that. We fail one another and, in repentance and restoration, we are made stronger and more humble. It is nice to have friends like that. Comforting. Restorative.

While we appreciate having a local, Reformed church, we do miss singing the psalms in public worship. Without intending to, I walked into a conversation where two church members were mocking those people who refuse to sing the hymns in worship. I was prostrate on the floor (not praying, but fishing out from under our chairs the crayons, notebooks, and an inappropriately attired Barbie doll, all evidence that the Butterfields Were Here).

When I emerged from the floor, shoving immodest Barbie in my purse head first, a man with kind eyes invited me into the conversation. "Rosaria, Sue tells me there are people here who won't sing because the hymns are man-made? Maybe our pastor shouldn't preach because he is using man-made words, after all, and not the pure words of the Bible! Ha!"

"I only sing psalms, Jack."

"Why?" he asked with a mocking grin that suggested he thought I was pulling his leg.

"Because of the Regulative Principle of Worship," I replied.

"The Regulating what?" He inquired.

The following Lord's Day, he apologized with great sincerity. I invited him to lunch with the heartfelt hope that we could talk about the different ways we interpret the Regulative Principle of Worship.

I appreciate this OPC congregation for many things, including the fact that I can disagree with people without giving complete offense. I also appreciate this church's faithful preaching and its special insight into adoption—as Christian doctrine and family-building. God has also built the pastor's family exclusively through adoption. When he offers the pastoral prayer, he prays for widows and orphans, as well as for the pregnant ladies in the congregation. I have heard too many pastoral prayers that effectively erase my children from the covenant, and I am grateful to worship in a church that sees God's majesty in adoption. I have never known pregnancy. But I have seen God move mountains in the lives of children, and use my very hands and heart to re-parent hurt and broken children, and this is the most powerful mission in my world.

Indeed, adoption is not only a powerful mission, but is also a central Christian doctrine. I think about this every day. Russell D. Moore penned a book entitled *Adopted for Life: The Priority of Adoption for Christian Families and Churches*. This is a book that I would buy by the case and send to every Christian pastor I know, if I could afford to do this. I especially love how he deals head-on with the accusation that adoptive parents are not "real" parents. Borrowing from J. Gresham Machen's book, *The Virgin Birth of Christ*, Moore says this: "if Joseph is not 'really' the father of Jesus, you and I are going to hell" (p. 67). He goes on to explain:

> Jesus' identity as the Christ...is tied to his identity as the descendant of David, the legitimate heir to David's throne. Jesus saves us as David's son, the offspring of Abraham, the Christ. That human identity came to Jesus through adoption. Matthew and Luke trace Jesus' roots in Abraham and David through the line of Joseph.

This provides another salient picture of how the real (material) is not always the true (Christ-infused).

Over the years, I have listened to too many grieving women who interpret their infertility as a sign that they cannot fulfill their God-given duty as a life-giver. One woman recently said to me: "I dreamed of having six children. When I didn't get pregnant in my first year of marriage, I felt betrayed by God because my dream is crushed." I find these conversations so fruitful for Christ-centered redirection. God is not crushing the dreams of parenthood when he deals the card of infertility. God is asking you to crush the idolatry of pregnancy, to be sure. And, he is saying: Dream My dreams, not yours! Currently, there are 7,000 children in Virginia who are waiting for adoption. Give him your dreams, and watch them become cosmic Christian doctrine. My role as life-giver is not compromised in any way by my infertility. My ability to see the world with spiritual eyes is sharpened by it, however.

Over the years, Kent has maintained his full-time job as a government contractor and served as pulpit supply for Reformed churches seeking a pastor. He served for seven months as full-time pulpit supply at another congregation. This small church even considered calling Kent as its pastor. We enjoyed learning and teaching with this small body. We celebrated the joys and liberties of psalm singing and delighted in offering Bible studies, prayer meetings, and fellowship meals in our home. Then, something happened. It often does. My testimony is like iodine on starch.

Someone I valued as a friend, a founding church member with influence, asked me what I would do if a homosexual entered our worship service. I quickly shared with her my testimony, apologizing that I hadn't done so earlier. I gave her a chapter of the book that you are holding in your hand and I asked her to read it and to let me know what she thought of all of this. A week later, she came to talk.

She took a deep breath.

All the color drained from her face.

She looked like she had just witnessed a crime scene.

Manifesting disgust and horror, she told me that she wished that I hadn't shared this with her. She quickly added, "Oh, I'm fine with this information, but X (another weighty founding church member) could never handle it. Do you have to tell people about *this*?" *This. Rosaria's unmentionable past.* Rahab the Harlot. Mary Magdalene. We love these women between the pages of our Bible, but we don't want to sit at the Lord's Table with them—with people like me—drinking from a common cup. That's the real ringer: the common cup—that is, our common origin in depravity. We are only righteous in Christ and in him alone. But that's a hard pill to swallow, especially if you give yourself kudos for good choices.

Fot years, I believed that Kent lost this pulpit because of my homosexual past. I believed this because affections cooled after my disclosure. I was relieved to learn after this book's publication that I was wrong. The search committee had other reasons. My friend's gut rejection still stung.

Sometimes people ask me if I feel like I am "wasting my life." It is a funny question, so odd that I don't know what to do with it. Their point is this: Because I am well educated, shouldn't I be doing "something" with it? It is hard to show—unless you come into my homeschool classroom someday—that I am still a professional at heart. My whole life, currently defined as a homeschool mom in the classical Christian tradition, relies daily on my educational training, and the discipline and intellectual rigor developed over the course of my life. I have had a complete life in school. I still read up to a hundred pages of something each day, translate something (these days, Latin), write papers, diagram sentences, and help students (my own children and others in my Classical Conversations community). I like to share with others what all English PhDs take for granted: fluency with words and their origins, the ability to parse any sentence at any time, an appreciation for the grammar of all fields of study, and a fearless embrace of broad reading lists.

Recently, my son had a friend over after school, and their conversation became a laboratory for me. My son has been homeschooled his whole life. His friend has always attended public schools. Here was their conversation:

Public School Boy: "All the girls at school *like* like, the boys. It is gross!"

Homeschool boy: "*Like*, like? I don't understand."

Public school Boy: "You know, *l-i-k-e*, like."

Homeschool Boy: "You mean 'like' is both a verb *and* an adverb?"

They abandoned this impasse for worm-catching, but here is what I noticed. Both boys are attending what we used to call grammar school (they are in the second and third grade). Grammar schools used to be places where children memorized the "grammar" (or foundational vocabulary) of academic disciplines: math, writing, reading, geography, history, and science. Traditionally, grammar school teaches the "pegs" of knowledge (as

Dorothy Sayers defines it in her provocative essay, "The Lost Tools of Learning"). The grammar of public schools, as defined by my son's friend, is the blossoming sexual desires of eight-year-olds. The grammar of my son's homeschool is the role played by parts of speech in sentence construction.

There is no question in my mind which grammar I want to teach in grammar school.

We had another encounter like this, one that also confirmed for me that I am not "wasting" my life.

Matt's adoption, in November 2010, became a huge celebration. In families like ours, adoption-days are shared by one and all. We got dressed up, went to the courthouse, and celebrated with hundreds of other families transformed by adoption in Loudoun County, Virginia. When we stepped into the courthouse, Knox, seven at the time, spotted a replica of the Magna Carta on the court room wall. He turned to Mary, four at the time, and said, "Cool! The Magna Carta." Together, they sang the history song about the Magna Carta that they had learned in Classical Conversations:

> English King John signed the Magna Carta in 1215, limiting the king's power. Later England's King Edward III claimed to be king of France and began the Hundred Years' War in 1337 (*Classical Conversations Foundations Guide*, 3rd Edition, p. 60).

In front of me, two social workers turned to each other and whispered, "Homeschooled."

This was an interesting encounter for a number of reasons.

The first reason was this: Learning for memory and retention and recitation is normal for us. Each week, my children learn at home a different history sentence (and Latin, geography, English grammar, science, and time-line one). We think this is normal and fun. For example, each history sentence tells something about the "who, what, why, where, and when" of significant historical events. Our motto in classical education is "train the brain to retain." Each week we learn to memorize these facts at home, and then on Friday, we join with our Classical Conversations community for a cooperative learning day, where my children are drilled in a classroom of eight children by their tutor in these subjects. They also participate in a large group fine arts project and a science project. As a normal part of life, my children learn real and vital things, and then share this learning with others for whom the learning bar is similarly high.

The second reason that my children's recognition and historical placement of the Magna Carta was significant is this: My children showed that they are keepers of the culture. They knew the significance of a cultural icon and could place it in history. Yes, they were once orphans. Yes, the same courthouse was used by God to confirm his providence and place them in a forever and covenantal Christian family. But even at four and seven, they knew that ideas have shape, form, and significance. The world is not swirling around them in the chaos of feelings and impressions. They memorize it. They steward it. It is, after all, God's world.

As I write this, the first sign of spring, my worm friend, is still with me on my writing table. It looks a little dry. I sprinkle some water from my cup. I hope it likes Perrier. There is another experience, though, of vital learning, from which our family is still recovering.

His name was J and he was a foster child placed in our home after Thanksgiving.

We first heard about J and his four other siblings on November 19, 2010, two weeks after Matt's adoption was finalized. The call came from Child Protective Services about a sibling group of five, all special needs, all found homeless in D.C. Social Services wanted us to take three boys: W (thirteen, autistic and mute, also described as "primitive"); J (eight, mentally retarded and mute); and K (seven, autistic, and mute). We learned that all of the children had been neglected, abused, and had witnessed the murder of one of their siblings by their mother's hand.

These stories are so gruesome and unfathomable. Just hearing them sears you in the crevices of your daily breath. How could any survive this?

Our home is not big enough for three additional children, so we declined and prayed. Providentially, we also had an elder's visit that night. (In the RPCNA, elders visit the homes of each church member yearly, to better understand how to shepherd the congregation.) That night, Pastor Steve and Elder T prayed for these children. All throughout the Thanksgiving holiday, my heart was heavy. I kept thinking about how sometimes the surplus of our lives prevents us from saying yes to those in need. You know, holidays are such busy times. When your calendar is too full, it squeezes out mercy ministry. It is hard to fit in the stranger and the outcast. By Friday, Kent and I both said to each other: "If Social Services calls again, let's try to say yes to one child."

The second call from Social Services came on Monday at 4:30 p.m. Mary had pinkeye and Knox had snot coming out of his nose in every color but clear. The social worker was tense. The children were at the agency already. The foster home that had said yes to the three boys decided that they could not handle them. The agency would close in thirty minutes. The question was simple: Could we take just one? I immediately told Knox and Mary what was happening and sent them into the dining room to pray. I was able to reach Kent on the cell phone and he said, "Yes, pick one." I joined Knox and Mary in prayer. Punctuated through daily, mundane prayers, for birthday parties and sick pets, was a request that God would bring this boy whose name we did not know to our home, help him to feel safe enough to talk, and help him to come to know Jesus. Listening to children pray is therapeutic. They made it sound so simple: Bring the child home, love him and feed him and pray for him, and do all with the faith that God loves orphans and he never gets the address wrong. I told my children that I was scared. The boy that God would send could not talk. How in the world could we communicate with him? Knox gave me *that* look and said, "Mom, kids talk with their eyes. We will understand him."

It all starts with the biggest hurdle, learning to say yes.

As soon as Kent got home, we piled in the van to pick up J. The office was closed by now. We met the social worker at the elevator and signed some papers. J came to us with eyes dilated and heart pounding, visibly through his shirt. He also had beautiful black eyes and a smile that could melt a Klondike Bar. Knox immediately had J laughing over something. In the van, the boys snacked on cereal bars and giggled over the book *Capyboppy*. But as soon as we got home, it became clear that J was terrified of dogs, cats, bathtubs, vacuum cleaners, doorways, darkness, and loud noises. He had no idea what to do with our back yard: the swing set, the dump truck, and the pile of dirt (a former garden patch gone to the dogs and the kids) were inscrutable.

My beloved neighbor Jane took our dogs, Sally and Bella, for a week while we introduced J to the myriad of other mysteries in the Butterfield home.

J did talk with his eyes, as Knox had said. But he also learned to talk with words. Kent predicted this would happen, perhaps out of self-defense in our house, where silence is a long-gone memory and where children even talk in their sleep!

J joined us for homeschool the first morning in our home. He was a diligent and able student. He proudly showed me that he knew all of his letters, that he knew how to spell his name (and that social services had misspelled his name on all his documents!), that he loved to draw and color, and that he loved to have books read to him. When Kent called at lunchtime, I said, "If J is mentally retarded, then I am too."

All of the children were sick and I was starting to get sick as well. Knox took over the bulk of the reading. J spoke his first audible word to Knox, as Knox started to read the book *My Truck is Stuck*. J looked at Knox in amazement and exclaimed: "You read!" From that moment on, J would find books around the house and bring them to any able reader. He loved books, and especially loved Knox reading to him.

J came to us with shoes that were two sizes too small and clothes with broken zippers. My mom went to Target for toothbrushes and pajamas and chicken nuggets for the week. My neighbor Michelle showed up at my door with *bags* of clothes and shoes and a winter jacket! J was thrilled! Each morning, he picked out dressy clothes: khaki pants and collared shirts. Matt gave J a watch, which J put on every morning. We witnessed how much J wanted to be clean and wear clothes that made a good appearance. Matt's watch on J's wrist was an interesting touch. Time and place meant something to J. I don't know how I would have dressed J without my mom and Michelle's contributions; I don't know how I would have gotten him to relax without Jane taking the dogs for a week; and I don't know how J would have learned to talk without all the children surrounding him with stimulation, love, and acceptance.

Soon, we fell into a routine. Morning Bible lessons and math and phonics, followed by lunch and exploration of the backyard. The backyard held many mysteries for J: Dirt to dig, Big Wheels to pedal and crash, and swings and slides all brought new weightless sensations and new things to learn. I have never seen my backyard as a place of mystery and intrigue in quite this way before. Next, we would come inside for art: finger painting, making letters and numbers with play dough, stamping a scene and then writing or dictating a story about it. During art lessons, J told us that he was scared of dogs because he was bitten by one and had witnessed a ghetto dog fight, where one dog had killed the other, leaving it a bloody, dismembered carcass.

After art and when Matt got home from school, our driveway became a basketball court. What a beautiful sight! J, Knox, and a gaggle of neighborhood boys, with Matt acting as referee or coach (even picking up a child and running him to the basket for a dunk), playing driveway basketball until it was too dark to see. After dinner, Kent played charades and Battleship with the children while I got the bathrooms ready for bath time. The whole time, J was relaxing and learning. I was mesmerized to behold the children in our neighborhood playing together as pieces of a puzzle assembled by God's grace and the feeble prayers of their parents.

My friend Martha came by often to give support and insight. Martha has been my mentor in many things, but mostly in my understanding of using compassion as the bridge to our hurt children. Compassion means "with suffering" and involves entering into the suffering of another in order to lead the way out. Martha had recommended a book to me that I was reading during my week with J. The book is called *The Connected Child.*[4] It was the guide that I needed. Parenting the hurt child means always knowing that you are parenting your emotional better, a human being who survived against all odds. In *The Connected Child*, the author uses this harrowing example: Imagine that the biological child you nurtured since birth was abducted at the age of four, abused, neglected, starved, and tormented, and then, miraculously, returned to you at seven. The author reminds the reader that you would do everything in your power to meet him at his place of hurt and bring him back to you. You would not go to an amusement park on his first day home or trundle him up for daycare and school during the first week. *Compassion. With Suffering.*

Both J and I got sicker as everyone else got better. Our routine became a little quieter. When I lose my voice (as I did this week), things get very quiet! The dogs came back on Saturday, and by then J was talking well enough to tell us what had happened and to listen as we told him that our dogs would not hurt him. Matt spent a lot of time showing J different features of the dogs. "Look at her paw pads! Sally's smell like popcorn. Here. Smell." Soon, J was carrying Bella (our nine-pound Shih-Tzu) around the house, stroking her, and saying, "You are so beautiful."

J loved his time with Kent. He was very accomplished at puzzles and even helped Kent by doing the hardest part of a 500-piece puzzle with very little help. He loved learning to play charades and Battleship. Kent was the parent who helped J with bath time and bathroom issues. Kent described J as a puzzle genius and the goodwill ambassador, and that he is!

J came to us mute, but who knows if this isn't a riddle of sorts: if the child screams in the ghetto and no one listens, how dare we really say that the child didn't scream?

J's social worker was working to find a home that would take J with his seven-year-old autistic brother. We started praying for God to raise up a Christian family for this dear boy. We hated to think of what might happen to a child like J in the welfare system and seriously considered whether we could be J's family. We knew, though, that we could not take two children. And we knew that if J was separated now from his siblings, it would be a tremendous loss for him and for the others. We worry about older children in foster care. For many people, an eight-year-old child of color with special needs is not the child of their mind's eye. There are no baby showers or MOMS Clubs for the adoptive parents of hurt and rejected children. Too often, children over the age of four just get bounced around from foster home to foster home or from foster home to birth families until the parents rights are terminated by the courts and the child is considered in the eyes of potential families "too old" to adopt.

We know that saying no to a child who needs a home is a risky thing. We prayed. We told the social worker that we supported finding a home that could keep some of the siblings together. We told the social worker that if this was not possible, then we would pray about whether God wanted us to adopt J. We left it at that and we prayed.

Then we got the phone call. A family in Woodbridge wanted to adopt both J and his seven-year-old brother. They had adopted a special needs sibling group before. They wanted younger children, but were willing to try with older ones. The social worker wanted me to let J know that he would be going to a new home. He would pick J up in thirty minutes. Could I have him ready to go by then?

I prayed. I sat down with the children and I asked J if he wanted to see his brother. His eyes beamed like I had never seen before. He smiled, he whooped, he jumped in the air. He was thrilled. Even Knox and Mary understood: It was good that J came and, now, it was good that J would go to someone else and be reunited with his brother. God gave us peace. I was especially glad that Knox and Mary had peace about this. As a family made up of adoption and foster care, the foundation of our lives together involves this bittersweet coming and going of children. Mercy ministry always comes down to this: You can help, but only Jesus can heal. This can be a tough lesson for adults, and a much tougher one for adopted children. Knox and Mary, though, have been cutting their teeth on this lesson since their earliest memory and showed real Christian peace and insight in letting J go. But now I wondered about J's future family. Were they Christians?

I packed J's things (all gifts from Michelle, Jane, and my mom) and then I sat down to write a letter to J's new foster mother. I started with Scripture:

> But whoever has the world's goods, and sees his brother in need, and shuts up his heart from him, how does the love of God abide in him? (1 John 3:17)

> For every creature of God is good, and nothing is to be refused if it is received with thanksgiving; for it is sanctified by the word of God and prayer. (1 Tim. 4:4)

I shared in my letter how I had prayed for a loving Christian home for J. I tore out pages from my journal that documented his progress during my precious week with him. I shared my daily schedule, included the portfolio of his work in homeschool, my assessment of his learning needs, and our family picture. I included my name and address and phone number. Then I signed and sealed the letter and prayed again.

J left and we all started to reassemble our house.
We felt like we were underwater.
Knox asked: "Will we ever know what happened to J?"
"I don't know," I said.
And then the phone rang. It was J's new foster mother. She read my letter and called immediately to tell me that God had answered my prayers—before I even prayed them. She and her husband are a Christian homeschooling family. J was reunited with his brother, and, now that J is speaking, there is hope for his brother, too. Over the years, the boys developed a wordless speech by making up hand signals that narrated to each other their terrifying private world. J's new mother was describing their interaction and how powerful it is that J can now speak for himself because now he can also speak for his brother. "Rosaria," she said, "God made a door for these boys when he taught J to speak words, and now J can lead his brother outside of their private hell."

Jesus is the word made flesh. We take the role of words for granted, we for whom literacy is as common as dirt. I don't think that we "taught" J how to talk that week. I know that a homeschool environment put him at ease and I know that he felt safe to "show what he knows" at a sunny kitchen table with books, letter boards, crayons, apple slices, and his favorite dinosaur sippy cup. I think that what really happened is that God sanctified and then answered our prayers. We prayed that J would talk, but God taught us to listen to and respond to a scared boy who at first talked with his eyes. Then, I think that when we learned to listen, it became safe for J to talk. That is, I believe, the bottom line of the Christian life. Jesus is the word made flesh, and our faith and our deeds of love puzzle together with the Lord of lords and King of kings setting the sequence that makes the pattern of grace-filled life.

It is time to move on.

This worm must go back into its burrow for a month or so. Dribbles of Perrier won't cut it any longer.

Hands must be scoured, dinner served, showers inaugurated, stories read, prayers shared, kisses exchanged, night lights turned on, and children tucked in.

We have, by God's grace, been given another day to serve and love, laugh and learn, pray and ponder. Spring is ready to burst into the open air, and we are ready to embrace it.

The children fell asleep quickly tonight.

Matt pulls into the driveway from the firefighter banquet. He is early, as usual.

As Kent and I go over the details of the day, the phone rings. It is the phone call we have been waiting for. Kent has been called to pastor a church. The vote from the congregation was unanimous. The call must be approved by two presbyteries before it is official, and as we wait and pray, the fervor in our house pitches to a high, joyful note.

Expanded Edition Features

Reaching Rosaria
The Lost Art of Hospitality

By Pastor Ken Smith

Floy and Ken Smith, with Dr. Rosaria Butterfield, 2013

While my wife, Floy, is from Louisiana and I was born in Vermont, we were brought together in the providence of God through the Christian ministry of the Navigators. Early in our Christian adulthood, we both learned from them the basic principles and disciplines of Christian discipleship. Floy heard about it at Northwestern Schools in Minneapolis. I was first exposed to their ministry when the Billy Graham Crusade came to Pittsburgh in 1952, which by this time had engaged Dawson Trotman and the Navigators to help follow up persons making decisions for Christ.

By the time Floy and I met and were married in 1956, we both knew and understood the fundamentals of Christian discipleship. LeRoy and Virginia Eims and children had come to Pittsburgh in 1953 and lived in my parsonage for two years. They were Navigators, and I learned by living in their family how God had designed the home environment as a place of warmth, fellowship, and growth. Floy had lived in the Trotman home in Pasadena, California before moving with them to the new and present headquarters of the Navigators in Colorado Springs, Colorado.

We were thus oriented to the home being the ideal place for Christian ministry to all kinds of people, starting, of course, with children. Today, in the gracious providence of God, our three sons and their wives walk with Jesus Christ, having led their children by godly example to worship God on a daily basis, and to do so as families. It is my hope that by sharing from our background as husband and wife and parents that you will understand that our experience with Rosaria in our home was simply routine for us.

Contact

"What led you to make contact with Rosaria?" I've often been asked that question. Following a weekend of a Promise Keepers rally in which many of our men participated with profit, Dr. Rosaria Champagne's article appeared in the Syracuse newspaper. Without downgrading the Promise Keepers' efforts unduly, she did make clear her priority that government programs address children's needs. One of our elders brought the newspaper to our elders meeting, threw it on the desk, and said, "We need to answer this." The assumption was that I as pastor would do it.

The article lay on my desk for some time. How does one answer such an article? Then I had an inspiration.

Ever since coming to Syracuse to pastor the Reformed Presbyterian Church there on South Salina Street, I had been burdened for the students nearby at Syracuse University, the "Orangemen." How could I get to them so that they would at least know what the Bible says—not merely to consider whether or not they believed it? That was my burden. And here was a university professor in the English department. She could understand my concern that these young lives know what's in a book, whether it was the Bible or not.

Now I had a strategy. I knew how to write my letter. I did not critique her article, but expressed my interest in equipping men. Then I posed my question. I asked if I could piggyback on this letter to ask her how a local pastor could see to it that the university graduates would know what the Bible—the book most influential of all books in American history and culture—actually says.

Later I told our eldest son, Ken—at the time a professor in the School of Management at the Syracuse University, and incidentally an acquaintance of Dr. Champagne—that I had sent the letter.

He assured me that as a faculty member Rosaria would respond. And she did—by phone.

Conversation

She writes about that conversation in this book. She asked me basic things like: was I an evangelical, what did I believe about the Bible, did I take the Bible literally, things like that. I don't remember what her next question was—I had not yet recognized the fact that she was interviewing me. After having talked for at least a half hour, I suggested our "continuing the conversation in front of the fireplace after one of my wife's good dinners." She accepted. Here was a good contact with the English department of the university, and I would have opportunity to press my cause over dinner.

We have had people inquire why we bring strangers into our home for dinner. I've explained that already to some degree. It harks back to the biblical idea of hospitality. The Bible says we as Christians are to be given to or practicing hospitality. "Seek to show hospitality" (Romans 12:13). The word translated "hospitality" is literally "love of strangers."

We today live in such a busy, self-centered world we don't even have time for friends! Who has time to prepare dinner? It would make a much bigger impression on our children's future, I suggest, to be calling off most of their persistent sports idolatry to enjoy family dinner at home and to practice the "love of strangers" with such guests. Today's children know little or nothing of such an approach to community. And our churches wonder how to reach the lost. Reach them for what?

It may be my fatherly pride that now must assert itself, but I'd rather call it my pastoral burden. Our youngest son recently finished a doctorate at Reformed Theological Seminary in Orlando, Florida with his thesis to be this very point: the ministry of the small church to strangers, the hurting, prisoners, street people. When I read it, I was deeply convicted as to how far the church of today in the West has estranged itself from this kind of ministry. We wonder how we can experience church growth, but that is not the issue. The issue is, how can we minister the gospel to hurting people?

God taught Floy and me in our early days that true discipleship looks to Jesus for growth. As Jesus calls us—including Rosaria—

to himself, he will build his church. Our mission is to do what Jesus did: give himself to the love of strangers.

During that first meal with Rosaria, we fell in love with her in no time. As she describes our conversation, we could talk about anything. Our desire was to get acquainted. That means a good bit of listening. And we listened.

It was an answer to one of Floy's questions that informed us that Rosaria belonged to the lesbian community. We kept right on talking. I wanted to get to the university students through her. It was in the course of that conversation, however, that she said, "I'm really not sure I know what I believe." I heard that! I wondered immediately whether she, rather than the university students, was the one God was leading us to. As it turned out, that was what the Lord was doing: opening up a friendship between us that would grow and blossom.

Content

In the fulfillment of Christ's commission to the church, the subject is the gospel of Jesus Christ. Paul the apostle asks his rhetorical questions in Romans 10, which boil down to this: "How can they believe in Him of whom they have not heard?" Winning a hearing is always the focus. I wanted to win a hearing with the university students. Rosaria wanted to screen that, and I happily responded when she volunteered to be a class of one over dinner at her house. My presentation is a forty-minute book review of the entire Bible focusing on its one message: the kingdom of Christ. Once I had presented that to Rosaria, I relaxed and waited on the Lord. But, as she writes, she had already in her research set about reading that Book.

One aspect of this whole saga should not be missed. The Lord was using many more people than Floy and me to meet Rosaria's many inquiries. One night following a panel discussion at the university library during which Rosaria and I were on opposite sides, a young man from our congregation during the question period addressed his query to Dr. Champagne. It was a very intelligent question, and it caught her attention. She asked me afterwards who he was and indicated she'd like to talk more to him. I arranged that by inviting them both to dinner at our home.

Floy and I said very little that night. That man knew her intellectual problems, had been there himself, and could respond to them as a Christian. I could not have done what he did that night. And it's important that one's personal problems that stand in the way of a clear faith in Jesus be addressed. That often takes time. When we understood where Rosaria was coming from intellectually, we allowed the Holy Spirit to take his time in bringing about the reorientation and repentance Jesus requires. Dr. Clyde Narramore once said in my hearing, "It's always good to let the Novocaine take effect before pulling the tooth." So we prayed and waited.

We knew Rosaria was reading her Bible, and by now it went beyond her scholarly research. She was being personally caught up by the Holy Spirit. Then one day she came to our Sunday worship service. Some have wondered about our not inviting her to church, and she mentions that. That was not an oversight. We knew she'd be expecting that, so we didn't need to. Further, I am a bit slow about inviting some people to our worship services. It is a long distance for a 21st-century pagan to a biblical worship assembly. We are often not geared to such persons, nor are our worship services. In some ways that's not strange. A worship assembly is the gathering of God's redeemed people. It is geared for them to express their worship to the living God. This involves a godly mind-set with accompanying vocabulary. It is very strange to one unacquainted with it. We decided to wait until Rosaria through our friendship was moved by the Spirit to come. And come she did! And we, of course, were gratified. And she never quit. She was now feeding on the Word of God and growing in grace — and mixing with a Christian community.

Church

The fellowship of a congregation in many ways becomes the drawing card for those who are being called by God to true salvation. Some think it is the preaching. Sometimes it is. But people "Stop, Look, and Listen," like the old sign at railroad crossings. Generally people do it in that order when they enter a church. Some surveys have said that newcomers decide within twenty minutes whether or not to return. Syracuse Reformed Presbyterian Church was a good environment into which to bring newcomers. Yes, we had our unusual ways, and there is always an orientation to a new setting. What I mean is that when Rosaria came to worship, Floy and I celebrated, having a bit of understanding of what this change of environment must mean to her as well as to us.

Rosaria also shares in her story how she used to come to our home on Sunday evenings for our small-group gathering. She often stayed long after everyone else had gone, and we talked. One night she seemed to be ready to commit her life to Christ. I asked her if she was ready, and she affirmed she was. We went to our knees in our living room and the three of us prayed. I don't look on this as her "moment" of conversion, for she had been in process for some time. It just seemed appropriate. It was another step forward in response to God's call in Christ.

Since she was closely tied in with her lesbian community — and let me tuck in here that we learned a great deal from her about that community — I was concerned that without undue delay she make the step into her new community, the church. Her old friends had, to a large extent, withdrawn from her and she needed the enfolding care of Jesus' community. She understood; so early one afternoon we talked about the meaning of church membership. So many questions came to her probing mind that I finally said, "Rosaria, you should read the Reformed Presbyterian *Constitution*." I do not suggest this for everyone; but from her questions I knew she could handle it and would not be satisfied until she had. She called me that evening about 6:30 and said she had read it and had twelve pages of questions! So I said, "Come on over and we'll discuss them." By 10:30 that night she was ready to assent to the Covenant of Church Membership. When she met with the elders, she shared her story — thirteen typed pages — I had asked her to prepare; and when she was finished we were all weeping. She took the covenant and was received.

Continuity

Anyone who knows anything about Christian conversion recognizes that confession of Christ is only the first step. In 1952 I heard Billy Graham say that coming to Christ was about 5%; growth to maturity, 95%. Rosaria has effectively reflected on the rough ground she traveled in the days following her public profession. What she calls a train wreck is not unusual for new believers, and it underscores the great need for intimate and faithful discipleship. Our love for and delight in Rosaria as our adopted daughter in the faith did not flag as she struggled with the damage. We kept in close contact and endeavored to keep our home open for any of her former community who needed love and shelter.

As she unfolded the next chapters of her new life in Christ, fairly soon she moved to western Pennsylvania where she found shelter and encouragement from colleagues of ours. And this is my opportunity to give thanks to God for those many others who have played a significant role in Rosaria's life and growth. The body of Christ is a marvelous organism where the life of Christ fills His saints so that they are able to build up one another in Christ, as Ephesians 4 describes. A good number of people in Beaver Falls, Pennsylvania understood that and gave themselves to enfold her in Christ-centered love and fellowship.

It was no small matter to us when God united Rosaria with Kent Butterfield! We were delighted. Never having had any daughters, I was deeply moved when I was asked to give Rosaria away in the marriage tradition when she and Kent were wed. And I did. In another sense Floy and I have never given her away but have kept her in our hearts as one of the great blessings of our life in Christ. To God be the glory!

Conclusions

Are there lessons to be learned from this conversion experience for your own ministry? I tried earlier to let you know something of Floy's and my lifestyle out of which flows our ministry. You can work on your own lifestyle, not to imitate us, but to evaluate whether or not your schedules and routines have space for "strangers." You can do something about that and begin to cultivate friendships with those not naturally like you. And to begin, pray that God will lead you to someone who needs what you have to give in Christ.

Recognize again that "salvation is of the Lord," as stated in Jonah 2:9. When I learned in early days of ministry that my fruit flowed from my union and communion with Christ, He gave me a new confidence in his using me as his servant to affect others' lives. That meant that, for effective ministry, my daily walk with

Christ was crucial. Jesus gives the ministry! That principle is universal. If you want that kind of ministry, then abide in Christ as he said in John 15.

Be a friend to your own children. Many youth have told me over the years in my ministry that they don't really know their dads. Some parents warned me about the coming teen years of our sons. They wouldn't describe it; they only said, "Just wait!" May I gratefully say that we are still waiting. Discipleship begins with your children, and our testimony is that our sons became our best friends during their teen years. It's that kind of environment of open, friendly and joking fellowship into which you can invite the stranger. Many have never seen a happy family! This is one of the greatest, and I might sadly say, unused evangelistic means the church possesses. Just have a happy family into which you invite others. They'll come back.

Finally, let's get over being stand-offish to people who are not like us. And here let me be open about the gay and lesbian community. In many ways they, as a movement, are indeed a threat to our society's stability. But, on the other hand, these are the people who need Jesus. Let me point out that people, according to the Bible, come in only two "sizes": saved sinners or lost sinners.

The person who is a lost sinner has a problem with *sin*. That is, he is under God's wrath and curse, at alienation with God, an enemy of truth and righteousness. His relationship with God is warfare! And until one bows down to God in humble confession and commits himself in faith to Jesus Christ, he will never be reconciled to God. That's the essence of sin: rebellion against the living God. The saved sinner, on the other hand, struggles with *sins* (plural). He now walks with Christ, but by the same faith seeks grace to overcome remaining habits and failures as the Spirit works to conform him to the image of Christ.

What does this mean in practice? I do not spend time talking with a non-Christian about his sins. That's not his problem. His problem is his *sin*: his broken relationship with God.

Can you now recognize why it was no problem for us to invite Rosaria to our home and table where we could talk about God and coming to know Him personally in Jesus Christ? Of course, we walked slowly, for we wanted her to know what it means experientially that "God so loves the world." (And, by the way, we did not know anything about her lifestyle when we invited her to dinner. Nor would it have mattered.) We can love sinners. Jesus fraternized with sinners but, sadly, was criticized for doing so by the religious hypocrites. But aren't we glad Jesus cares for "the stranger" to grace?

There were no calculated techniques employed in our contact with Dr. Champagne other than seeking to be friendly as followers of Christ. But is that a technique?

Our Shared Journeys
Hospitality Helped Bring Us Together and Then Became a Priority in Our Life as a Couple

By Kent Butterfield

Rosaria and husband, Kent

I was not raised in a Christian home. One night as I lay in bed, too lazy to turn on the light, I searched for my favorite rock station on the radio (I still like some rock and roll). Instead, I lit upon a Christian sermon, heard the gospel for the first time, and was intrigued enough to tune in to this channel, night after night.

After a few weeks, I became a closet Christian. Too frightened to tell any of my unbelieving family and friends, I led a double life: Christian in the closet, heathen in the world. (Rosaria and I share some good jokes about my time in the closet.) After two years, my mother caught me reading the Bible for the very first time. After I left for college, I decided to come out of the closet and find a church!

My first experience attending church while a student at the University of North Carolina–Chapel Hill was not a positive one. This large Bible church boasted over 600 souls each week. In a year of attending, not once was I approached by anyone.

Hospitality did not exist towards me, this lonely Christian who had no spiritual direction, mentor or oversight.

The next church I found myself in was over an hour away and met in someone's basement in a beat-up part of town. An elder and his wife had us "college kids" over for lunch each week. That first lunch consisted of balancing a Styrofoam plate of messy food on my left knee, a cold iced tea in the left hand, and swatting flies with my right hand. Still, I felt the kindness and Christian love.

Soon we were handed off to the new family at church. This family did not have much but certainly expected us to come over each Lord's Day for fellowship and a meal between morning and evening services. This family showed sacrificial love in inviting me and others into their home week after week, and I had no idea of the hardship it involved. The bonehead of the group (myself) did not know the family struggled to make ends meet. It was only years later that I learned abut the great sacrifice this family offered to open their home to us each week for a year. These weren't just meals they offered me. Hospitality ministry provided the comfortable space I needed to confront any number of questions: How could God love me and allow my father to die when I was nine? What does Jesus require of me as a Christian? Why do I need to be a member of a church or be baptized? No one had ever talked to me about membership and baptism. I thought that attendance and tithing sufficed.

I was convicted of my sin in the safest place in the world: a meager living room under the canopy of Christian hospitality.

But a troubling matter developed when I heard the pastor talk. He used this same living room to let his guard down and to gossip. Words reveal the heart. I heard him talk with some other older members about having his knife ready when he traveled to a certain area and saw "porch monkeys." The pastor was from rural New York State. I have never heard that term before or since, but it etched its way into my memory, and it revealed that he lacked love. He was a pastor who lacked love for all men. I left this church for another, and then another. Each time I came or went, I learned more about hospitality, doctrine, my Lord, and my heart.

The first church I actually joined was an Orthodox Presbyterian Church in Raleigh, N.C. The founding pastor was a gentle, dedicated, and orthodox grandfather figure from Iowa. He was the living, walking twin of General Robert E. Lee, and his name was Cromwell Roskamp. (It is ironic that years later I joined the Reformed Presbyterian Church of North America, which traces its roots to Scotland and the Covenanters, who were defeated in battle by Oliver Cromwell.) Pastor and Mrs. Roskamp sponsored the midweek prayer/Bible meeting in their home. After praying, Mrs. Roskamp offered a special meal to all, as if each person there was her most prized friend. She spared nothing and served the best that she had. This degree of hospitality overwhelmed me at the time. I wanted to decline, knowing that this banquet was served at a sacrifice. In the Roskamps' home I learned the importance of giving and taking, of sharing resources and needs.

I learned during these years that God truly loves a cheerful giver and that those cheerful givers more readily express their love towards God with a thankful spirit. Those who testify to God's abundance of blessing in their lives (firstly, spiritual blessings) more freely give of their resources to others. Grumblers and complainers have quick reasoning why they cannot help out and be involved in ministry.

Living as a single adult, I experienced the privilege of extending hospitality toward others when I was part of a small—really small—church plant. People often overlook the hospitality gifts of single Christians. God used Christian hospitality so formatively in my own life that I was grateful to be on the giving end at last. I was living on $16K a year and I knew food was costly, but I could not limit food for hospitality or gas for travel to church. It was the other frills of life I could cut back on or not indulge. Hospitality and fellowship were too important for me. This is what I needed for my own sanctification.

I met Rosaria when she taught at Geneva College. It was routine to see her hosting eight or more college students in her small one-bedroom apartment. After we got married, we never had to discuss whether we would have people over. Hospitality was the backbone of our shared journeys to Christ, and we were (and are) eager to share it with others. As a wedding present, someone gave us a guestbook. During our first year of ministry, we fed more people meals and had more overnight guests than there are days in a year. After that, we stopped keeping track of the numbers, because we didn't want to let the numbers set the bar. We want Christ to set the bar. Year after year, the Lord has blessed our hospitality ministry, even now with children and full-time pastoral ministry. It always comes back to the home.

When we were first married, money was tight. We had a thriving ministry to the singles in the church where I interned. We would pray and provide what we had. God used many others to help. One night an elder from our church stopped in front of our house, popped open the trunk, and started stocking our freezer with meat and vegetables. God just put it on his heart to do this, even though this was as much a sacrifice for him as it would have been for us. There was no stopping him.

We left Beaver Falls for Northern Virginia, and there found a college ministry and a church plant with no other house to meet in but our own. As Rosaria found herself cooking for forty to fifty people each Lord's Day and countless others throughout the week, I found myself teaching people Reformed theology on the one hand and how to drive a car on the other! College is a confusing time for Christians, and our house was an extended example of applied theology. Some days our house looked like a hospital. Other days it looked like a *Little House on the Prairie* knitting class. Some days our house sounded like a seminary or a university classroom. It is amazing to see Rosaria balancing crock pots and bread pans while unfolding the pitfalls of Marxist ideology and German Romanticism for our contemporary culture.

Our new meeting place was near a Christian college that did not serve breakfast or lunch on the Lord's Day. We want our student members/visitors to keep the Lord's Day holy and not require people unduly to work for them, but my wife was also concerned about starving college students. Coffee cake, fruit and coffee awaited the students and visitors at church. I would have to tell people to stop talking and eating, for we were ten minutes behind in starting! (Why do people complain a pastor does not end in time when they, the congregants, do not sit down in time to start at the designated hour?)

Then the Lord sent us children—many children over the ten years we were foster parents in Virginia. That added another layer of love, loss, care, and fellowship to our hospitality ministry.

We have found having people over allows them to relax and unwind and open up more than they would at church. Many times we had wonderful discussion as I taught through the *Westminster Larger Catechism*. This book offers a majestic breadth and depth about God's character and our Christian responsibilities. Sometimes we didn't read anything at all. Instead, we talked about the sermon. This can be a little threatening from the pastor's point of view, but I have always survived! Reading *Pilgrim's Progress* together or studying mercy ministry or even psalmody provided many challenges to people's convictions, sentimentality and Bible understanding.

We always balanced this reading and talking with *doing*. In all of my pastorates, we have developed relationships—deep, abiding, and real—with people in the local nursing home and within the community. Recently I preached a series on hospitality and how it impacts evangelism, mercy ministry, and supports the church ministry overall. I believe it is easier to encourage all of this in the setting of hospitality. The influential southern theologian of the 19th century, R. L. Dabney, remarked that more teaching is done by the pastor outside the pulpit than in the pulpit. I have found that to be true time and time again.

Letters from Rosaria

Two Open Letters

Letter from Rosaria to my brothers and sisters in Christ who have gay and lesbian friends and family:

Dear Friend,

Perhaps you are reading this because someone you love has just come out to you as gay or lesbian, and, truth be told, you wish that she hadn't told you. Perhaps you wish that things could just go back to how they used to be. Perhaps you wish that you could just have your little girl back, or your spouse or your brother. But God has given you an even greater gift. He has given you the gift of knowing the truth. God has given you the gift of knowing exactly how to pray. Even if you do not know how to talk, how to think, and how to prepare for the future, if you are Christ's own, you know how to pray. And, we can never go back. "Back" does not exist, in God's economy. We must go forward, through the valley of the shadow of death, and behold the spiritual table and banquet that God has prepared, the table in the presence of your enemies, where he promises overflowing sustenance for today. Do you see this table? Dare to peek. Will you try to go there?

This information about your loved one may feel like a terrible blow. Maybe a public stoning. Don't waste it. Don't waste your stoning. Take my hand and let's travel this journey together. Let's go to the throne of grace, as children of the King. Let's go to the table, the bounty, the safe space in enemy territory.

God is still God, even in these confusing times. Christ still places a light yoke on his people (Matthew 11:25-30). Christ still bears the burden that we cannot carry. Christ still kept God's law fully, thus securing the perfect righteousness that is imputed to us by faith alone (Romans 3:21-26; 2 Corinthians 5:21). Christ purchased us with his own blood. By grace alone, he gives us the yoke of gratitude for salvation—even as the whole world crumbles around you. This Christian joy is a bloody joy, to be sure; and a light yoke does not promise an easy life. You may feel now, more than you ever have, that the "afflictions of the righteous are many." Maybe you feel the pinch of this spiritual truth right now as you hold this book in your hands. Maybe you feel the pain of suffering for the "upward call" that Paul mentions in Philippians 3:13.

Then sit down a spell. Have a good, long, drink from the living waters. Roll the promises of God through your fingers like the yarn that daily travels across my knitting needles. Savor this: "For he spoke and it came to be; he commanded, and it stood firm" (Psalm 33:9). Remember that "God's saying is doing. His promises are one with his performance of them. He is just as willing to perform as to promise. There is no distance between his saying and doing, as among men" (David Clarkson, *Works*, Vol. 1, quoted in my favorite devotional, *Voices from the Past: Puritan Devotional Readings*, p. 194. Buy this book now and read it daily. You will thank me for this advice). Even now, in the midst of the valley of the shadow of death, God calls you to feed on his faithfulness, not on the bile of your worldly doubt (Psalm 37:1-8). You are what you eat, especially now as you stand in the gap for your loved one.

Standing in the gap is rigorous business, and it helps to clarify the issue, the sin, and the enemy. It helps to know whom you can trust. It helps to remember that all sin displeases God and that homosexuality is not a special sin. It helps to remember that repentance unto life has already been secured through Christ's resurrection for those who put their trust in him alone. It helps to remember that the only orientation in the Bible is that which marks the eternal weight of the soul, which will last forever. It helps to remember that you did not cause this sin, this shame, this unbearable-on-your-own-strength moment. It helps to remember that we were all "born this way" in the original sin of Adam's federal headship, even as the adjective "this" references different proclivities for different people. Different and the same. A million ways to shatter the image of God, and one way to restore it. Like a stained-glass window or mosaic that shows the edges of alien color and texture, we are all broken and made whole in the same way, by the same blood.

It helps to remember that Jesus will never leave you or forsake you, if you have put your trust in him. It helps to remember that Christians are given supernatural allies in times of trouble. Faith is a gift from God to you and a lens through which to make meaning of today. That's right. Faith is a lens of discernment, not an ornament or accessory that comes and goes. Faith strengthens us, gives us concealed provisions to bide and brook public shame. It produces palpable promises ringing in tidings of joy in the desolate wasteland of grief. Faith unfolds providence in proportion to God's unfailing love. You can do this. You can love your God with all your heart, soul, strength and mind, and your gay and lesbian friend as well. There are no lines to draw. Homosexuality is a sin, and God is bigger than any sin and any grief.

Yes, homosexuality is a sin, but so is homophobia. Homophobia is the irrational fear of a whole people group, failing to see in that group God's image diminished but not extinguished by sin, and that God's elect people linger there, snared by their own sin and awaiting gospel grace. It is an act of homophobia to believe that people in the LGBT community are either too sinful to respond to God's call on their life, or to believe that people in the LGBT community have a fixed nature that will never, according to the blustering, unfounded, and uncharitable declarations of secular psychology, change by the power of God's command. What does God change? Our heart. That is where it all starts.

Yes, sexual sin has a searing quality to it, and we live in a world that abounds with sexual sin. Is homosexuality really more fixed in practice than masturbation or pornography? I doubt it. Homosexuality simply has a political lobbying agency. Don't be sucker-punched by that. God is the same yesterday, today and tomorrow; and the Bible's truth, its inspired and inerrant integrity, did not somehow overlook a whole people group in its ordinances about sin and grace. It is an act of homophobia to declare sexual orientation a fixed feature in a person's life. People have choice sins—we all do—and we all must go to war with them. The Bible calls these sins "indwelling" because they take root and residence so deeply below the surface that they define us—if we allow. We must pray like the psalmist: "Lord, all my desire is before you" (Psalm 38). All my desire. Not just part of it. So, sin is sin, indwelling sin especially deceptive, and our loved one is vying to get us to see this from his or her point of view. But if we are Christ's purchased own, we must see this through Christ's point of view. It is the only point of view with "equity" (Psalm 98:9).

For Christ's sake and the sake of your loved one, we must remember what Christ's victory means: death to sin, especially the ones that wrap themselves around our necks. In the resurrection, Jesus gave sin an irreparable blow. Even our choice sins have been given a death warrant. Oh they may linger for a while—like a decapitated chicken—but the undisputed end is death. With true repentance God promises true redemption. New creatures in Christ (2 Corinthians 5:17). God promises that he will give your loved one the capacity and joy in living lives of holy sexuality. For some, that will mean celibacy. For others, that will mean redemptive heterosexuality. God knows what we need, and he loves your child or friend more than you do.

Don't travel this journey alone. Tell your pastor and your elders. If you are a Christian and you need a local church, find one. The Church is Christ's bride, and you will find community and power there, to pray, to serve, and to love in equity.

These words that I write here are my promise and pledge to pray daily that the stronghold of sexual sin will be broken, for your loved ones and for mine, for Christ's name and God's glory.

So, what should you do?

First, you should apply yourself to all of the means of grace available to you: prayer, Bible reading, psalm singing, worship, taking of the sacraments. Get to know the Bible more intimately today than you have ever known it. Memorize whole chunks at a time, and ask a friend in the Lord to memorize with you.

Second, start a thanksgiving list. We are to be thankful in all things, even our trials. Keep a journal, marking down three things each day that call your heart into thanksgiving to God.

Third, serve in your church. You may be broken, but you are not dead (yet), so renew your strength in service to God's people.

Fourth, keep the lines of communication open with your loved one. Love and listen. Find neutral turf and stand together on something that matters to you both.

Fifth, take the log out of your own eye daily, remembering that repentance is the posture of a Christian. Then, if you have sinned against your loved one, ask forgiveness.

Finally, keep a journal of this season of prayer. Write down not only your petitions, but also all of the ways that God remembers his covenant with his people as found throughout the Bible. Start in Genesis and read all the way through Revelation. Use a good commentary, such as *Matthew Henry's Commentary of the Whole Bible*, to take along as a good friend. Pick up a good devotional, such as *Voices from the Past: Puritan Devotional Readings*, to focus and sharpen your spiritual eye. Remember that even in this heavy trial you may offer to God the sacrifices of praise. Renew your hope, and link arms with others who need you to view this trial through the eyes of faith.

Letter from Rosaria to my friends who are in the LGBT community:

Dear Friend,

Perhaps you are reading this because someone gave you this book in the hope that it will "fix" you. If so, you likely think that I have three heads and you understandably want to throw this book in the garbage. I would feel the same way. Or perhaps you think that I am a hypocrite. After all, I was "only" in lesbian relationships for ten years, and prior to that, I lived a heterosexual life. Perhaps you feel that I am misusing my past and misrepresenting yours in the process. That is not my intention. My story is not representative or diagnostic. If people are using my testimony in this way, they should stop (and I will tell them that, if you need me to).

My time in the LGBT community was defined by my affiliation with feminist and queer theory worldviews that endorsed the power of choice in sexual practice, and the process of fluidity in sexual identity. The spiritual battle for me rested in pride, not sexual lust. I wanted to define myself apart from male authority, and at the same time I wanted to enjoy the company, community, and symmetry of lesbian sexuality.

After years of meeting with Pastor Ken and Floy Smith, Christian neighbors, members of the Syracuse Reformed Presbyterian Church, and after years of reading and fighting with the Bible, the Bible simply got to be bigger inside me than I. This sounds daft, I know. But the Christian faith is supernatural. By faith in Christ through the free gift of God's grace, the Holy Spirit slowly but surely filled my soul with an alien sensibility, one that called me to a deep sense of my eternal belonging to a holy God. I started to see the Bible as the table of contents of my life. And I started to see how my pride (which manifested itself in my lesbianism) separated me from the holy God who made me and promised to take care of me. I didn't stop feeling like a lesbian, not at first. Rather, I started to feed on the promises in the Bible and spend more time embracing the means of grace than the means of the world. God slowly and powerfully changed me. I don't mean here that God changed me from gay to straight. The blood of Christ is too powerful to merely reflect status-shifts in identity or sexuality. God made me to see myself in the context of his love, his design, his authority, his sovereignty, his salvation, and his holiness. I saw that in my pride, I was persecuting Jesus himself, the one and only source of atoning love.

God changed my whole life. My repentance was not a simple, singular, past-tense thing. The Holy Spirit led me to repentance in kindness, not shame. My sin was that I was persecuting Jesus by failing to love him best. All of the other issues were shadows and types of that sin. I lost my friends and my community. But he preserved my soul, renewed my hope, and restored my meaning and purpose, even in the midst of great turmoil and grief. Because God made me to see that if I was set apart from before the foundations of the world to love and obey him, resistance was impossible.

That the Bible is a supernatural book and that God is a living life force is daily palpable to me. It is true and you can trust it. I loved my LGBT friends (and still do). But I love God more. God changes us—all of us. It is not just people who identify as LGBT whom God calls to change. The Christian life is the relinquished life—for all or for none. And sin is sin.

Sin never feels bad—not unless it is accompanied by great affliction (like a car crash following drunk driving). The Bible calls sin deceptive because it deceives us to believe that it is harmless. This is true for all of us. We are all the same, and we are all in the same boat. The reason that sin is bad is because it displeases God. And the only way that we know this is because the Bible says it. The Bible is true, inspired (literally "God breathed"), inerrant (no errors), and written by a loving God who anticipates every problem and pain we have. It is the table of contents of our whole lives—all of us. The Holy Spirit in kindness calls us to repent of sin. All sin does is prove that God was right all along. There is no shame in love like that. And in repentance and faith, God recreates us and our worlds: He restores our relationships, renews our hopes, and remakes our lives. We live in peace, knowing that a holy God purchased us by his blood, knowing that the Bible daily speaks truth, blessing, and courage into our hearts, and knowing that through faith and repentance (both gifts from God, not things that we manufacture), God hears and answers our prayers.

This isn't some "pray the gay away" imbecility. God isn't Santa Claus and your pet sin isn't a Hello Kitty toaster. So, if you haven't already thrown this book in the trash, please keep reading. Better yet, get a Bible and read it instead of this one. (I like the NASB translation.) And please pray that the Lord will lead you to a local church where you can talk these things out with folks who get it.

Frequently Asked Questions

1) What moved you to write *The Secret Thoughts of an Unlikely Convert*?

I wrote the book so I could remember and keep close the details of the inner landscape of my conversion to Christ. I wanted to remember, and pass on to my children, the rugged terrain and sweet joys.

2) Some people have said that you would sell more books if you didn't get into the details of your post-conversion experience. Why was it important to you to include that?

After God saves you, your alarm rings, you swing your feet out of bed, and you face—square on—the details of the sin that led you to the Cross and the redeeming blood of Christ that covers those sins. But, there you stand. You have to do something. The latter chapters of the book tell you what I had to do, what I felt called to do, how God led me in one direction and then another.

The worldview conflict was this: I went from being someone who felt that I was responsible and entitled to interrogate the Bible to someone who believed that the Bible had authority over my life and therefore had the responsibility and entitlement to interrogate me. That truth—that the Bible interrogates me—does not stop with conversion. Therefore, the post-conversion issues raised in *Secret Thoughts* are in some ways proof of the fruit of Christian living, insofar as they reveal a heart searching to have the Bible interrogate it. Indeed, if Christians do not demonstrate to a watching world our willing submission to the

Lord, and our understanding that we do not have it all together, but rather, require daily washing in the word and daily repentance, why should anyone take our testimony seriously?

Homeschooling, and foster- and adoptive-parenting are not gospel-imperatives. They are, for me, ways that the Lord has put his fingerprint on me. They have transformed my world, enlarged my heart and prayer life, and put matters of public sin and grace in heartbreaking perspective. Psalm singing is gospel dynamite and I am glad for the chance to share it with my readers.

The bottom line: I don't write with an eye to fashion or popularity. I write from the best that my mind and my heart can give. I don't presume that we will all agree.

3) Some people who read your book struggle with some of the very issues you did. Where can such a person find support?

Secret Thoughts was written for a Christian audience. I figured that about twenty people in my small, unknown denomination would purchase it, in much the same way that people might buy a church cookbook because they like the minestrone soup recipe that I had in the soup section. When the book started to break out of my tiny, obscure world, my life opened up in ways that I could not have anticipated. One amazing joy has been that many of my friends in the LGBT community—old and new ones—are reading *Secret Thoughts* and talking with me about God's call on the lives of his people.

When I started meeting with Ken and Floy Smith and reading the Bible, I had a faithful church praying and waiting for me. I also had faithful Christian neighbors—Ken and Floy. I had people who loved me enough to tell me the truth. They loved me enough to make sure that the Bible in its entirety had full reign in our conversations and our relationship. They showed me good practices—daily Bible reading, psalm singing, family devotions—and kept me accountable to them. They showed by example what a life looked like that allowed the Bible and its teachings to interrogate it. They showed me by example what godly sacrifice looks like. They did not sugarcoat God's call on our lives, his claim on our identity (and sexuality), and the many treasures he gives us here on earth as well as in the life after this one. They made me know that there is no isolation in the Christian life. I was welcome, with all of my struggles, to join them. They did not act as if I was polluting them with my struggles or my questions. They showed me that real Christian living means leaning hard on the Bible and on Christ, on applying our faith as a life condition (the just shall live by faith). They also helped me to see that our job in this life is to listen to God, not listen to yourself.

So, in summary:

It really helped me to have a few good friends in the church to whom I could run, at all hours of the night and day.

It helped to know that the crushing loneliness that seemed to be obedience's first fruit could be broken in the time it took to dial the phone.

It helped that when I called these inner-circle friends, they didn't jolly me out of my problems, but guided me into deeper repentance.

It helped that these were orthodox Christians and therefore they didn't say, "There is no sin in your feelings; God just made you that way."

It helped that these friends believed in an Almighty Christ, one who changes his people at the root. My inner circle was not satisfied by the illusion of safety of some insular Christian culture that had no real impact on the world in which we lived. They believed—and I did too—that only total abandonment to Jesus could heal what ails us.

Once I found my Christian sea legs, it also helped to step out in faith and become an "out" Christian in a parallel fashion to which I had been an "out" lesbian. It helped because of the way the Lord fills you up when you do this. Sometimes we think, using the logic of the world, that caution is the best practice. In God's economy, this is not true. The best way to feel the Lord's presence, to experience his comfort, and to taste the sweetness of the promises of salvation's fruits here on earth is to take personal risks for his glory. Public repentance of public sin proves that God is a faithful and true witness to his creation. There is no shame in that.

4) What have been helpful practices for you in following Christ?

Daily and long Bible reading, psalm singing, prayer meetings, fellowship of the saints, rolling up your sleeves and helping people who cannot (yet) help themselves, worshiping the Lord, memorizing the *Westminster Shorter Catechism*, reading and applying the *Westminster Confession of Faith*, and taking communion as often as possible (at the First Reformed Presbyterian Church of Durham, we have weekly communion).

The most helpful biblical principle is that God wants us to be "complete and well" (Psalm 41B, verse 12). "And thus am I sustained by You to be complete and well, And in Your presence evermore, You make me safely dwell." The most helpful family worship text for me is Doug Comin's *Family Worship Helps*.

5) As a Christian, how can I be better at reaching out and being a friend to those who do not agree with my convictions?

Ephesians 4:29 says, "Let no unwholesome word proceed from your mouth but only such a word as is good for edification according to the need of the moment, so that it will give grace to those who hear." The line "need of the moment" is important. Too often in our relationships, we feel as though we must speak our full heart on all matters. We feel dishonest if we don't spell out the whole story of gloom and doom when we see people we love making dangerous decisions. We panic, say more than we ought, and then justify this as honesty. We would do well to show ourselves people who value humility, gentleness, and patience, as Jesus does with us. We also should not fear learning from people who think differently than we do, and welcoming the chance to dialogue across these differences. Finally, we must be very careful about thrusting private conversations into public venues. Real heart changes happen in private, not public, spheres.

6) What are some good practices for Christians who struggle with same-sex attraction (SSA)?

Live as a faithful member of a Bible-believing church, meeting for worship, prayer meetings, fellowship, and Bible studies.

Cultivate honest accountability in your church, asking for prayer and checking in with your pastor or elder or someone known to your pastor for accountability and encouragement.

Know your enemy: Besetting and indwelling sexual sin is predatory. Therefore, have no contact with pornography or with secret lovers—physical, non-physical, virtual, or real.

Do not misuse Christ by asking him to baptize your feelings; instead, ask Christ to fill up your heart and soul and thereby create your feelings.

Cultivate honest friendship and kinship in your church community. Practice hospitality. Don't isolate. Your church needs you. You are not damaged goods. If you are in Christ, you are the Son or Daughter of the King.

Remember that temptation is not a sin, but you should not toy with it or let it define you.

Psalms

Psalm singing is a daily means of grace that I love, embrace, and practice. When I don't know where to turn, I open up my psalter. You always know where God is in your suffering when you sing the Psalms. In the Psalms, God breaks down the steps of your faith pilgrimage. The Psalms take your brokenheartedness seriously. God gave them to you as a love letter to show that he made you and takes care of you. As you sing the Psalms, you hear your broken vulnerability and God's omnipotent accompaniment.

The following are some of the psalms that were particularly meaningful to me during the years recorded in this book.

If you need help with psalm singing, go to www.psalter.org.

—Rosaria Champagne Butterfield

How Blessed the Man

Psalm 1

For in Him we live and move and have our being.
—Acts 17:28

1. ¹How blessed the man who does not walk Where wick-ed men would
2. ³He shall be like a grow-ing tree That's plant-ed by the
3. ⁴But yet the wick-ed are not so; They are like chaff that

guide his feet, Nor stands in paths with sin - ful men, Nor
wa - ter-side, Which in its sea - son bears its fruit, And
blows a - way. They will not in the judg - ment stand, Nor

sits up - on the scorn-er's seat. ²The LORD's law is his
has a leaf that does not fade. In all that may his
sin - ners with the righ-teous stay. The LORD the way of

great de - light, His med - i - ta - tion day and night.
hands em - ploy, He will pros - per - i - ty en - joy.
just men knows; The wick - ed to de - struc - tion goes.

Gauntlett's Comprehensive Tune Book, 1851

GIESEN 88.88.88

Psalm 1B taken from *The Book of Psalms for Worship* © 2009
Crown & Covenant Publications, 7408 Penn Ave., Pittsburgh, PA 15208-2531.

Within Your Tent Who Will Reside?

Then Jesus called a little child to Him,
and set him in the midst of them. — *Matthew 18:2*

1. ¹O LORD, with-in Your tent who will re-side?
2. ³He will not harm his friend, nor him de-fame;
3. He keeps his prom-ise, though it brings him pain.

And on Your ho-ly hill who may a-bide?
He will not seek to spread his neigh-bor's shame.
⁵His gold no prof-it earns from wrong-ful gain.

²Who walks in blame-less-ness, Who acts with righ-teous-ness,
⁴But vile men he ab-horred, And rath-er would a-ward
No bribes will he re-ceive, The guilt-less to ag-grieve;

His heart will truth ex-press— It is his guide.
To those who fear the LORD, An hon-ored name.
Those who such things a-chieve Un-moved re-main.

Robert Lowry, 1826–1899

LOWRY 64.64.66.64

The Lord's My Shepherd

Psalm 23

I am the good shepherd. The good shepherd lays down His life for the sheep. —John 10:11

1. ¹The LORD's my Shep - herd, I'll not want; ²He makes me down to lie In pas - tures green; He lead - eth me The qui - et wa - ters by.
2. ³My soul He doth re - store a - gain; And me to walk doth make With - in the paths of righ - teous - ness, Ev'n for His own name's sake.
3. ⁴Yea, though I walk in death's dark vale, Yet will I fear no ill; For Thou art with me, and Thy rod And staff me com - fort still.
4. ⁵A ta - ble Thou hast fur - nished me In pres - ence of my foes; My head Thou dost with oil a - noint, And my cup o - ver - flows.
5. ⁶Good - ness and mer - cy all my life Shall sure - ly fol - low me; And in GOD's house for ev - er - more My dwell - ing place shall be.

Jesse S. Irvine, 1872; desc. W. Baird Ross, 1871–1950

CRIMOND CM

How Blessed Are All Who Fear the LORD

The promise is for you and your children. Psalm 128
— *Acts 2:39*

1. ¹How blessed are all who fear the LORD, And
2. ³Your wife with-in your house will be A
3. ⁴Be-hold, thus shall the man be blessed Who
4. O may you see, through-out your days, Je-

walk with-in His ways. ²You'll eat your la-bor's
vine whose fruits a-bound; Your chil-dren will as
tru-ly fears the LORD. ⁵The LORD from Zi-on
ru-s'lem pros-per well. ⁶May you your chil-dren's

fruit with joy, And pros - per all your days.
ol - ive plants Your ta - ble gath - er 'round.
give to you His bless - ing and re - ward.
chil - dren see. Peace be on Is - ra - el!

African-American melody; adapt. Henry T. Burleigh, 1939; desc. Walter Sturlaugson, 2006   McKEE CM

Bibliography

Endnotes

1. Charles Bridges, *Proverbs: A Geneva Series Commentary* (Carlisle, Pa.: Banner of Truth, 1846, 1998).

2. Rick Warren, *The Purpose Driven Life: What on Earth Am I Here For?* (Grand Rapids, Mich.: Zondervan Press), 2002.

3. David Engelsma, "Marriage, The Mystery of Christ and the Church: The Covenant-Bond in Scripture and History (Jenison, Mich.: Reformed Free Publishing Association), 1998.

4. Karyn Purvis, David Cross, and Wendy Sunshine, *The Connected Child.* (New York: McGraw-Hill), 2007.

Resources
Books on Adoption and Foster Care

Adoptive Familes. Bimonthly journal. www.adoptivefamilies.com

Boss, P. *Ambiguous Loss: Learning to Live with Unresolved Grief.* New York: Routledge Press, 1999.

Brodzinsky, A. B. *The Mulberry Bird.* Indianapolis, Ind.: Perspectives Press, 1996.

Clark, Nancy A. and B. Bryan Post. *The Forever Child: A Tale of Anger and Fear.* www.foreverchild.net; www.bryanpost.com. 2003.

——. *The Forever Child: A Tale of Lies and Love.* 2002.

——. *The Forever Child: A Tale of Loss and Impossible Dreams.* 2005.

Eldridge, Sherrie. *Twenty Things Adopted Kids Wish Their Adoptive Parents Knew.* New York: Dell, 1999.

Fahlberg, V. *A Child's Journey Through Placement.* Indianapolis, Ind: Perspectives Press, 1991.

Hersch, Patricia. *A Tribe Apart: A Journey into the Heart of American Adolescence*. New York: Fawcett Columbine, 1996.

Krementz, Jill. *How It Feels to be Adopted*. New York: Alfred A. Knopf, 2001.

Lowell, Pamela. *Returnable Girl*. New York: Marshall Cavendish Press, 2006.

McCreight, Pamela. *Parenting Your Adopted Older Child*. Oakland, Calif.: New Harbington Press, 2002.

Munsch, R. *Love You Forever*. Buffalo: Firefly Books, 1986.

Riley, Debbie and John Meeks, *Beneath the Mask: Understanding Adopted Teens*. Case Studies and Treatment Considerations for Therapists and Parents (CASE). Silver Springs, Md.: C.A.S.E. Publications, 2005.

Hall, Beth and Gail Steinberg, *Inside Transracial Adoption*. Indianapolis, Ind.: Perspectives Press, 2000.

Books on Christian Living, Theology, and Worldview

Beeke, Joel R. *Parenting by God's Promises: How to Raise Children in the Covenant of Grace*. Sanford, Fla.: Reformation Trust, 2011.

Bridges, Charles. *Proverbs: Geneva Series of Commentaries*. Carlisle, Pa.: Banner of Truth Press, 1846, 1998.

Bridges, Jerry. *Trusting God Even When Life Hurts*. Colorado Springs, Colo.: NavPress, 1988.

Burroughs, Jeremiah. *The Rare Jewel of Christian Contentment*. Puritan Paperbacks. Carlisle, Pa.: Banner of Truth Trust, 1648, 1998.

Bushell, Michael. *Songs of Zion: A Contemporary Case for Exclusive Psalmody*. Pittsburgh: Crown & Covenant Publications, 1977. 3rd edition, 1999.

The Catholic Encyclopedia. Appendix to The Holy Bible, The Catholic Press, 1954.

The Constitution of the Reformed Presbyterian Church. Pittsburgh: Crown & Covenant Publications, 1989.

Edwards, Gene. *A Tale of Two Kings: A Study in Brokenness*. Wheaton, Ill.: Tyndale House Publishers, 1980.

Horton, Michael. *God of Promise: Introducing Covenant Theology*. Grand Rapids, Mich: Baker Books, 2006.

Keller, Timothy J. *Ministries of Mercy: The Call of the Jericho Road*. Second Edition. Phillipsburg, N.J.: P&R Publishing, 1997.

Lloyd-Jones, D. Martin. *Spiritual Depression: Its Causes and Its Cures*. Grand Rapids, Mich.: Eerdmans Publishing Company, 1965, 1980.

Lundgaard, Kris. *The Enemy Within: Straight Talk about the Power and Defeat of Sin*. Phillipsburg, N.J.: P&R Publishing, 1998.

Meyer, F. B. *The Shepherd Psalm*. Chicago: Fleming H. Revell Company, 1889.

McLaren, Brian D. *A New Kind of Christian: A Tale of Two Friends on a Spiritual Journey*. San Francisco.: Jossey-Bass Press, 2001.

Miller, C. John. *Repentance & 20th Century Man*. Fort Washington, Pa.: Christian Literature Crusade, 1975, 1998.

Moore, Russell D. *Adopted for Life: The Priority of Adoption for Christian Families & Churches*. Wheaton, Ill.: Crossway Books, 2009.

Palmer, Parker J. *A Company of Strangers: Christians and the Renewal of America's Public Life*. New York: Crossroad, 1986.

———. *The Courage to Teach: Exploring the Inner Landscape of a Teacher's Life*. San Francisco: Jossey-Bass Publishers, 1998.

Pearcey, Nancy. *Total Truth: Liberating Christianity from its Cultural Captivity*. Wheaton, Ill.: Crossway Books, 2005.

Pohl, Christine D. *Making Room: Recovering Hospitality as a Christian Tradition*. Grand Rapids, Mich.: Eerdmans Publishing Company, 1999.

Ryle, J. C. *Holiness: Its Nature, Hindrances, Difficulties, and Roots*. England: Evangelical Press, 1879, 2001.

Schwertley, Brian M. *Sola Scriptura and the Regulative Principle of Worship*. Southfield, Mich.: Reformed Witness, 2000.

Selvaggio, Anthony. *What the Bible Teaches About Marriage*. England: Evangelical Press, 2007.

Sire, James W. *The Universe Next Door: A Basic Worldview Catalogue*. 3rd ed. Downers Grove, Ill.: InterVarsity Press, 1997.

Smith, Peter Wallace. *The Open Door of Christian Hospitality*. Unpublished dissertation. 2010.

Tripp, Paul David. *Age of Opportunity: A Biblical Guide to Parenting Teens*. Phillipsburg, N.J.: P&R Publishing, 1997.

———. *Instruments in the Redeemer's Hands: People in Need of Change Helping People in Need of Change*. Phillipsburg, N.J.: P&R Publishing, 2002.

Vanhoozer, Kevin J. *Is There a Meaning in this Text? The Bible, the Reader, and the Morality of Literary Knowledge*. Grand Rapids, Mich.: Zondervan Press, 1998.

Vos, Johannes G. *The Westminster Larger Catechism: A Commentary*. G. I. Williamson, ed. Phillipsburg, N.J.: P&R Publishing, 2002.

Welch, Edward T. *Blame It on the Brain? Distinguishing Chemical Imbalances, Brain Disorders, and Disobedience*. Phillipsburg, N.J.: P&R Publishing, 1998.

Williamson, G. I. *The Westminster Confession of Faith (For Study Classes)*. 2nd edition. Phillipsburg, N.J.: P&R Publishing, 1964, 2004.

Warren, Rick. *The Purpose Driven Life: What on Earth Am I Here For?* Grand Rapids, Mich.: Zondervan Press, 2002.

Watson, Thomas. *The Doctrine of Repentance*. Puritan Paperbacks. Carlisle, Pa.: Banner of Truth Trust, 1668, 1999.

Books on Feminism and Cultural Studies

Kintz, Linda. *Between Jesus and the Market: The Emotions that Matter in Right-Wing America*. Durham: Duke University Press, 1997.

Kintz, Linda, and Julia Lesage, eds. *Media, Culture and the Religious Right*. Minneapolis: University of Minnesota Press, 1998.

Books on Hermeneutics and Postmodernism

Althusser, Louis. *Lenin and Philosophy and Other Essays*. Trans. Ben Brewster. New York: Monthly Review Press, 1971.

Gould, Stephen Jay. *Rocks of Ages: Science and Religion in the Fullness of Life*. New York: Ballantine Books, 1999.

Lacan, Jacques. *The Four Fundamental Concepts of Psycho-Analysis*. Jacques-Alain Miller, ed. Alan Sheridan, trans. New York: W. W. Norton & Co., 1973, 1981.

Laplanche, J. and Pontalis, J. B., eds. *The Language of Psychoanalysis*. Donald Nicholson-Smith, trans. New York: W. W. Norton & Co.., 1973.

Homeschooling

Bortins, Leigh A. *The Core: Teaching Your Child the Foundations of Classical Education*. New York: Palgrave MacMillan, 2010.

Favorite Cooking Resources

Cook's Illustrated: www.cooksillustrated.com

Cooking Light: www.cookinglight.com

Cuisine: www.cuisine.com

King Arthur Flour Catalogue: www.kingarthurflour.com

Penzey's One: www.penzeysone.com

Other Titles Available from
Crown & Covenant Publications
www.crownandcovenant.com

The Book of Psalms for Worship

Called "a psalter for the 21st century," this is a hymnbook comprised of all 150 psalms of the Bible, useful for singing in personal devotions, groups, and public worship.

Refuge and Communion (recordings)

Selections from *The Book of Psalms for Worship* (above) sung by a choir of the Syracuse Reformed Presbyterian Church. Available as downloads or CDs.

Free psalm download each month at www.crownandcovenant.com

Singing the Songs of Jesus: Revisiting the Psalms

The Psalms were composed for singing. Despite renewed interest in psalm singing, few books explain how the Psalms function as hymns for Christ-centered worship. *Singing the Songs of Jesus* fills that gap without shying away from difficulties, like the doubts and curses of the Psalms. This book shows why the Psalms are suited for Christian praise and how to use them for powerful and relevant worship.

Can God Accept You?

Pamphlet explaining how a person can receive acceptance and forgiveness by God.

The Gospel & Sexual Orientation

This small book provides guidance on the subject of homosexual orientation, not simply about the scriptural, scientific and moral issues, but also guidance for care and counsel to someone who believes their identity is homosexual. It interacts with contemporary scholarship and holds the Scriptures in high esteem, but also presents a model of how to care for and walk alongside a person who is struggling with his or her sexual identity.